LETTERHEAD
& LOGO
DESIGN 11

First published in the United States of America by
Rockport Publishers, a member of
Quayside Publishing Group
100 Cummings Center
Suite 406-L
Beverly, Massachusetts 01915-6101
Telephone: (978) 282-9590
Fax: (978) 283-2742
www.rockpub.com

Library of Congress Cataloging-in-Publication Data available

ISBN: 978-1-59253-761-7

10 9 8 7 6 5 4 3 2 1

Design: Design Army, Washington DC

Printed in Singapore

LETTERHEAD & LOGO DESIGN 11

BEVERLY MASSACHUSETTS

ROCKPORT PUBLISHERS

DESIGN ARMY

CONTENTS

DREAM BIG, START SMALL.

Design Army was founded on a simple principle: Dream big, start small. We believe in simplicity. In fact, you could say that it's part of our identity. Our logo is a star. Our colors are red, brown, and mint green (and sometimes, upon request, a really ballsy yellow). We use one typeface. It's simple, consistent, effective—all the things you'd expect from a powerful brand. Simplicity is perfection. And to us, the 400 identities in this book are the perfect expression of pure, singular ideas. Of course, that kind of simplicity can be hard to come by. To get to the finalists in this book, we spent more than two weeks evaluating over 5,000 entries from all over the planet. Along the way, we confirmed what we already knew: It's the little thoughts that have the biggest impact. They inspire us to push farther. They work harder. They last longer.

SO, JUST HOW BIG CAN ONE LITTLE IDEA BECOME?

SMALL IS HUGE.

HOACHLANDER DAVIS PHOTOGRAPHY, LLC

TYPOGRAPHIC

DESIGN FIRM
Blok Design
ART DIRECTOR
Vanessa Eckstein
DESIGNERS
Vanessa Eckstein
Mariana Contegni
Patricia Kleeberg
CLIENT
Evolutia

DESIGN FIRM
Red Design Consultants
ART DIRECTOR
Rodanthi Senduka
DESIGNERS
R. Senduka
A. Angelopoulos
CLIENT
Courouzos

DESIGN FIRM
3group
ART DIRECTOR
Ryszard Bienert
DESIGNER
Ryszard Bienert
CLIENT
Fundacja Pro Arte

DESIGN FIRM
Default
ART DIRECTORS
Anisa Suthayalai
Alex Lin
DESIGNERS
Anisa Suthayalai
Alex Lin
CLIENT
Merge Architecture

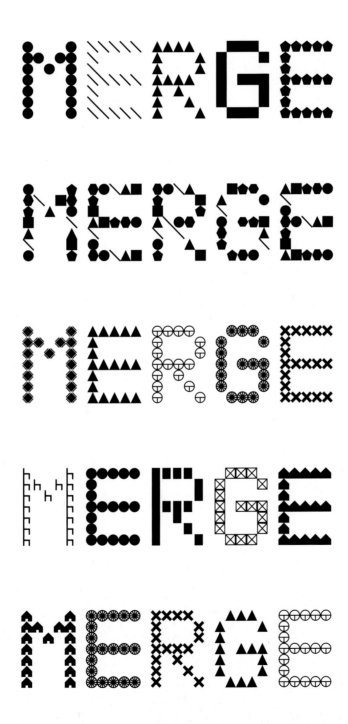

DESIGN FIRM
Boccalatte Pty Ltd.
ART DIRECTOR
Suzanne Boccalatte
DESIGNER
Dave Balletti-Collins
CLIENT
Penrith Performing
& Visual Arts

DESIGN FIRM
True story.
DESIGNERS
Eric Wagner
CLIENT
True story.

Beneath the surface of communication lies a series of considerations that shape its...

Stirred by its surface, the recipient was curiously compelled to investigate the package's concealed contents.

True story.

1801 W Larchmont Avenue Unit 201 Chicago Illinois 60613

True story.

1801 W Larchmont Ave Unit 201 Chicago Illinois 60613
Phone 773 244 8148 Cell 773 636 8888 eric@truestoryinc.com

True story. 1801 W Larchmont Avenue Unit 201 Chicago Illinois 60613 Phone 773 244 8148 Cell 773 636 8888 www.truestoryinc.com

1 **DESIGN FIRM**
Oxide Design Co.
DESIGNERS
Drew Davies
Joe Sparano
Adam Torpin
CLIENT
Quantum Market
Research

2 **DESIGN FIRM**
Deniz Marlali
ART DIRECTOR
Deniz Marlali
DESIGNER
Deniz Marlali
CLIENT
SAPKA
Hat by Aysel

3 **DESIGN FIRM**
Pink Blue Black
& Orange Co., Ltd.
ART DIRECTOR
Siam Attariya
DESIGNER
Siam Attariya
CLIENT
Boy Thai Band

4 **DESIGN FIRM**
Wink
ART DIRECTOR
Scott Thares
DESIGNER
Scott Thares
CLIENT
Target

5 **DESIGN FIRM**
Studio Output
DESIGNER
Ben Atkins
CLIENT
Ministry of Sound:
Resident DJ

6 **DESIGN FIRM**
Default
ART DIRECTORS
Anisa Suthayalai
Alex Lin
DESIGNERS
Anisa Suthayalai
Alex Lin
CLIENT
Readymade Projects

1

šâp̃ǩà

2

Boy Thai

3

backyard
discovery

4

5

Croft
Cafe

6

DESIGN FIRM
Design Ranch
ART DIRECTORS
Michelle Sonderegger
Ingred Sidie
DESIGNERS
Michelle Sonderegger
Tad Carpenter
CLIENT
360 Architects

1 DESIGN FIRM
5Seven
ART DIRECTOR
Clint Delapaz
DESIGNER
Clint Delapaz
CLIENT
5Seven

2 DESIGN FIRM
Rethink
CREATIVE DIRECTORS
Ian Grais
Chris Staples
DESIGNER
Lisa Nakamura
CLIENT
Vancouver Sculpture
Biennale

5SEVEN

1

2

1 DESIGN FIRM
5Seven

2 DESIGN FIRM
Rethink

articulation e.V.

Artilleriestraße 6
27283 Verden
Telefon 04231/957543
Fax 04231/957400
info@articulation.name
www.articulation.name

articulation e.V.

Artilleriestraße 6
27283 Verden
Telefon 04231/957543
Fax 04231/ 957400
info@articulation.name
www.articulation.name

Kreissparkasse Verden
KTO . 19 004 571
BLZ . 291 526 70

this is our **letterhead**™

this is our **envelope**™

just to **say:**

this is my **card**™

I am the creative director

DESIGN FIRM
Blok Design
ART DIRECTOR
Vanessa Eckstein
DESIGNERS
Vanessa Eckstein
Mariana Contegni
Vanesa Enriquez
CLIENT
Taller De Empresa

DESIGN FIRM
Turnstyle
ART DIRECTOR
Steve Watson
DESIGNER
Madeleine Eiche
CLIENT
Turnstyle

DESIGN FIRM
Foundry Creative, Inc.
ART DIRECTOR
Zahra Al-Harazi
DESIGNER
Kylie Henry
CLIENT
Metro Architecture

1 DESIGN FIRM
Pitch Creative

ART DIRECTOR
Tim Bridle

DESIGNER
Tim Bridle

CLIENT
Pitch Creative

2 DESIGN FIRM
Studio Cream
Design

ART DIRECTOR
John Valastro

DESIGNER
John Valastro

CLIENT
Head Over Heels

3 DESIGN FIRM
The Bradford Lawton
Design Group

CREATIVE DIRECTOR
Bradford Lawton

DESIGNER
Bradford Lawton

CLIENT
Greater San Antonio
Builders Association

1

HEADOVERHEELS

2

GREATER
SAN ANTONIO
BUILDERS
ASSOCIATION

3

DESIGN FIRM
Asli Kuris Design
ART DIRECTOR
Asli Kuris
DESIGNER
Asli Kuris
CLIENT
Ayse Ebru Tuner

S.A.R.
AYŞE EBRU TÜMER MİMARLIK OFİSİ

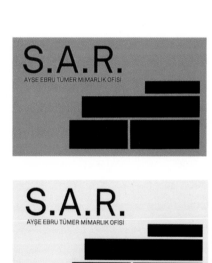 

Keleşharımı Mevkii Mimoza Sok.
Gardenya Sitesi No: 1 Türkbükü Bodrum

Tel 0252 377 5977
Faks 0252 377 6186

www.sar-aet.com

DESIGN FIRM
3group
ART DIRECTOR
Ryszard Bienert
DESIGNER
Ryszard Bienert
CLIENT
Andrzej Grabowski

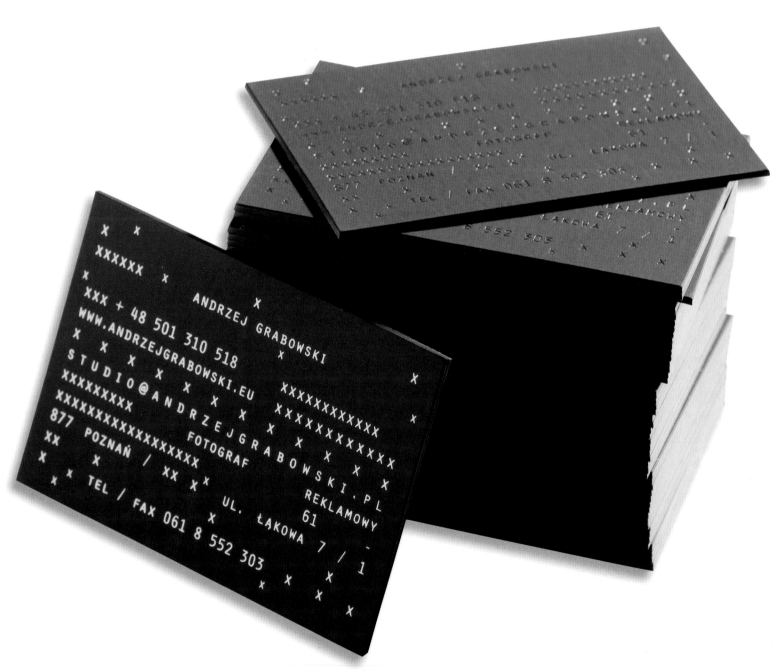

1 DESIGN FIRM
EMMI

ART DIRECTOR
Emmi Salonen

DESIGNER
Emmi Salonen

CLIENT
Emmi Salonen

2 DESIGN FIRM
LOWERCASE, INC.

ART DIRECTOR
Tim Bruce

DESIGNER
Tim Bruce

CLIENT
LOWERCASE, INC.

3 DESIGN FIRM
Timber Design Co.

ART DIRECTOR
Lars Lawson

DESIGNER
Lars Lawson

CLIENT
8 Fifteen

4 DESIGN FIRM
Luke Despatie &
The Design Firm

ART DIRECTOR
Luke Despatie

DESIGNER
Luke Despatie

CLIENT
Cream Productions

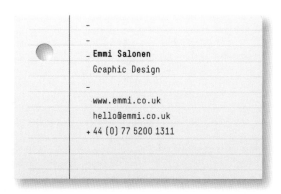

1

2

3

4

FORGET COMPUTERS®

N° ▦▦ 312 602 5345
HELP@FORGETCOMPUTERS.COM

1020 S. WABASH AVE. *Chicago* ILL.
60605-2255

FORGET COMPUTERS®

N° ▦▦ 312 602 5345
HELP@FORGETCOMPUTERS.COM

1020 S. WABASH AVE. *Chicago* ILL.
60605-2255

FORGET COMPUTERS®

N° ▦▦ 312 602 5345
HELP@FORGETCOMPUTERS.COM

BEN GREINER *Chicago* ILL.

FUNNEL : ERIC KASS
1969 SPRUCE DRIVE
CARMEL INDIANA 46033
UNITED STATES

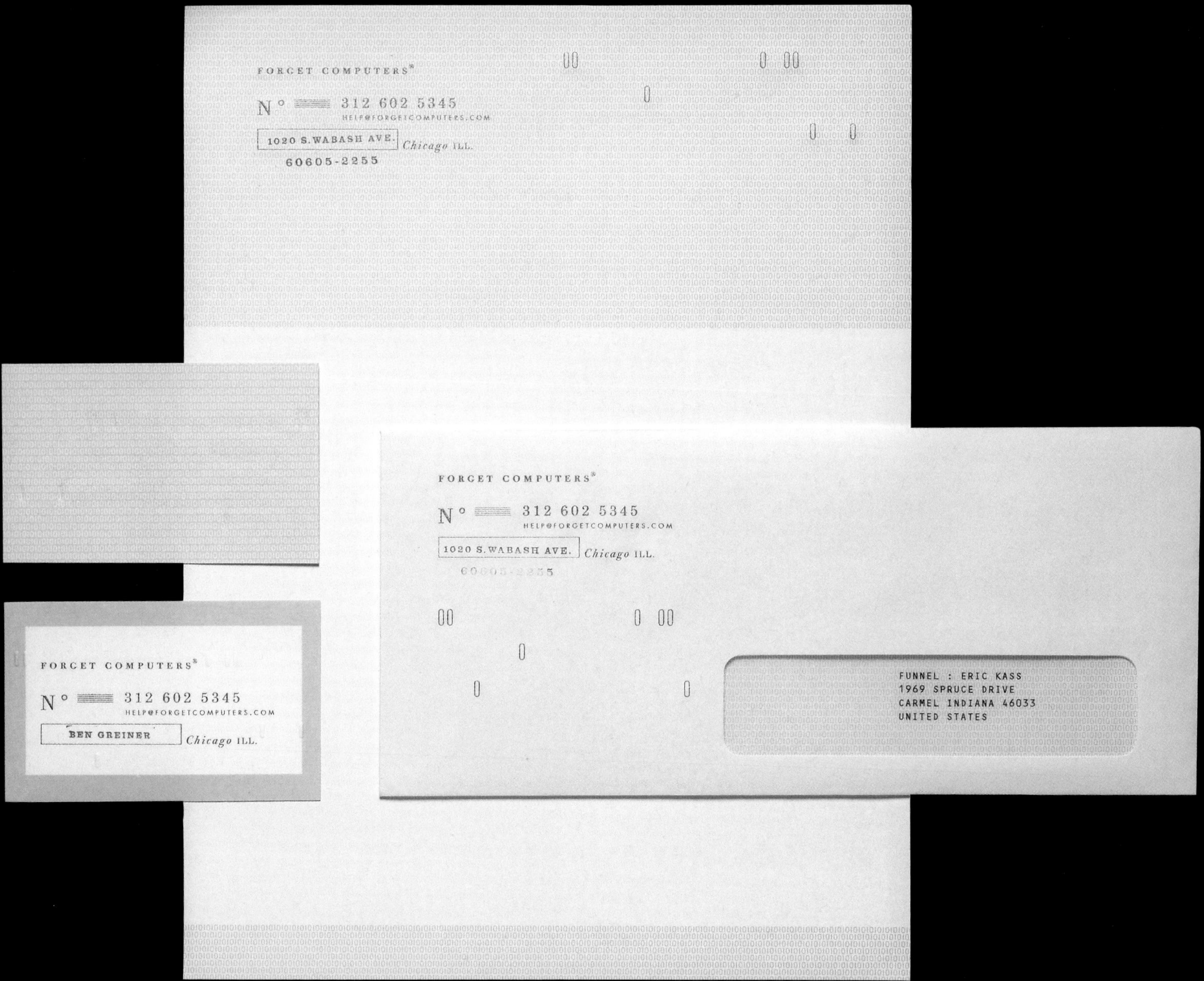

1 DESIGN FIRM
Tomko Design
ART DIRECTOR
Mike Tomko
DESIGNER
Mike Tomko
CLIENT
Six

2 DESIGN FIRM
Doug Fuller, Logo
& Identity Designer
ART DIRECTOR
Doug Fuller
DESIGNER
Doug Fuller
CLIENT
Doug Fuller

3 DESIGN FIRM
Skákala
ART DIRECTOR
Petr Skala
DESIGNER
Petr Skala
CLIENT
Connection

4 DESIGN FIRM
Turner Duckworth:
London &
San Francisco
ART DIRECTORS
David Turner
Bruce Duckworth
DESIGNER
Chris Garvey
CLIENT
Sonora Mills

5 DESIGN FIRM
Fresh Oil
ART DIRECTOR
Dan Stebbings
DESIGNER
Nelson Couto
CLIENT
Aka Restaurant

6 DESIGN FIRM
Default
ART DIRECTORS
Anisa Suthayalai
Alex Lin
DESIGNERS
Anisa Suthayalai
Alex Lin
CLIENT
Kid O

1

2

3

4

5

6

DESIGN FIRM
Blok Design

ART DIRECTOR
Vanessa Eckstein

DESIGNER
Vanessa Eckstein
Marianna Contegni
Patricia Kleeberg

CLIENT
Émigré Film

brandston partnership inc.

new york   beijing   shanghai

lighting design

brandston partnership inc.

lighting design

bpi

brandston partnership inc.

new york   beijing   shanghai

lighting design

bpi

122 West 26th Street, 5th Floor New York, New York 10001

bpi

122 West 26th Street, 5th Floor New York, New York 10001
P.212.924.4050 F.212.691.5418 www.brandston.com

Lindsay
photographer
Siu

108 West 1st Avenue Vancouver British Columbia Canada V5Y 1A4
>> TEL 604 708 0304 >> FAX 604 708 0308 >> CEL 604 765 4567
>> info@lindsaysiu.com >> www.lindsaysiu.com

Lindsay
photographer
Siu

108 West 1st Avenue Vancouver British Columbia Canada V5Y 1A4
>> TEL 604 708 0304 >> FAX 604 708 0308 >> CEL 604 765 4567
>> info@lindsaysiu.com >> www.lindsaysiu.com

Lindsay
photographer
Siu

CONTENT:

ALL IMAGES COPYRIGHTED LINDSAY SIU PHOTOGRAPHER
108 West 1st Avenue Vancouver British Columbia Canada V5Y 1A4
>> TEL 604 708 0304 >> FAX 604 708 0308 >> www.lindsaysiu.com

Lindsay
photographer
Siu

108 West 1st Avenue Vancouver British Columbia Canada V5Y 1A4

DESIGN FIRM
Behaviour / Cadson Demak
ART DIRECTOR
Anuthin Wongsunkakon
Pongtorn Hiranpruek
DESIGNER
Sunida Shewtanasoontorn
CLIENT
D DNA Publishing
Company Limited

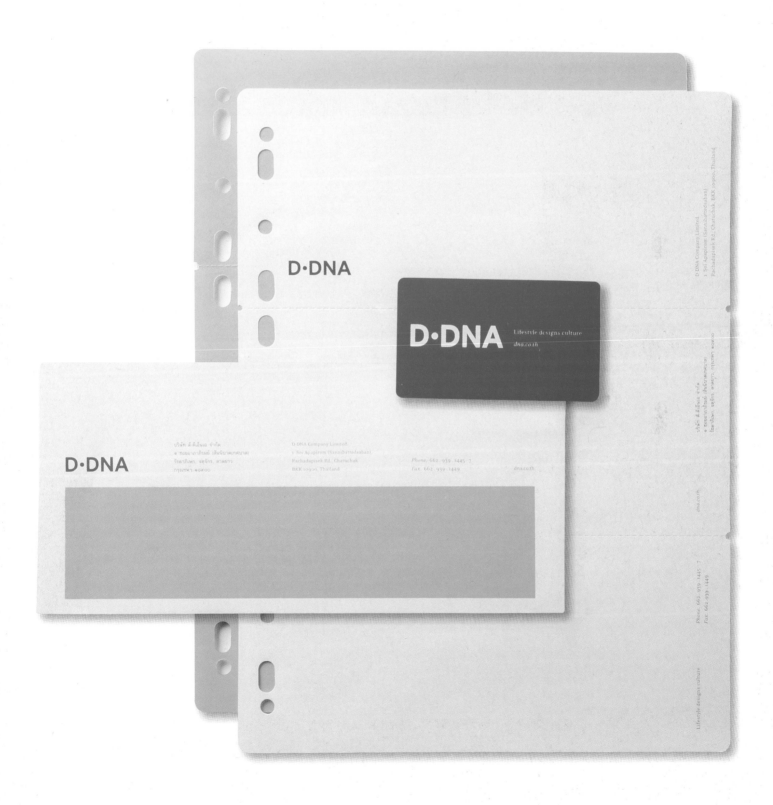

DESIGN FIRM
Public, Inc.

ART DIRECTOR
Todd Foreman

DESIGNER
Kim Cullen

CLIENT
Pfau Long
Architecture

DESIGN FIRM
Konnect Design
ART DIRECTOR
Karen Knecht
DESIGNER
Sarah Rainwater
CLIENT
John Demerritt
Bookbinding

DESIGN FIRM
White_Space
ART DIRECTORS
Aaron Evanson
Mark Masterson
DESIGNERS
Aaron Evanson
Mark Masterson
CLIENT
White_Space

white_space

DESIGN FIRM
LG2 Boutique
ART DIRECTORS
Cindy Goulet
Claude Auchu
DESIGNER
Cindy Goulet
CLIENT
Robitaille Photo

DESIGN FIRM
Design Army
ART DIRECTORS
Pum Lefebure
Jake Lefebure
DESIGNER
Lucas Badger
CLIENT
America Votes

AMERICA √OTES

1401 NEW YORK AVE NW, STE 720
WASHINGTON DC 20005
TEL 202 962 7240
FAX 202 962 7241
DIR 202 962 7272
CEL 202 360 5675

WWW.AMERICAVOTES.ORG
SBRUNO@AMERICAVOTES.ORG

SARAH BRUNO

ASSOCIATE DEVELOPMENT DIRECTOR

1401 NEW YORK AVE NW, STE 720
WASHINGTON DC 20005

TEL 202 962 7240
FAX 202 962 7241

WWW.AMERICAVOTES.ORG

AMERICA √OTES

1401 NEW YORK AVE NW, STE 720
WASHINGTON DC 20005

AMERICA √OTES

PAID FOR BY AMERICA VOTES AND NOT AUTHORIZED BY ANY CANDIDATE OR CANDIDATE'S COMMITTEE

BY ANY CANDIDATE OR CANDIDATE'S COMMITTEE

1 DESIGN FIRM
Alex Just Creative
ART DIRECTOR
Alex Just
DESIGNER
Alex Just
CLIENT
Procreative

2 DESIGN FIRM
Nope Advertising
& Design
ART DIRECTOR
Vlado Mazic
DESIGNER
Vlado Mazic
CLIENT
Nope Advertising
& Design

3 DESIGN FIRM
Design Army
ART DIRECTORS
Pum Lefebure
Jake Lefebure
DESIGNER
Taylor Buckholz
CLIENT
NCRG
(National Center for
Responsible Gaming)

1

2

3

DESIGN FIRM
Airside

ART DIRECTOR
Airside

DESIGNER
Airside

CLIENT
Airside

I've never been much of a letter writer. Copy for a financial institution's worldwide ad campaign... no problem. A mission statement for a pharmaceutical company's internal brand book... piece of cake. But a personal letter... not so easy. Brings up too many painful memories. Memories of my first love. She was perfect. I wrote her letters every day for three years straight professing my unwavering love. I even sent her my school pin, but no response. No notes, no cards, nothing. Damn you Farrah Leni Fawcett, we could have been so good together. **Paul Russell, BA LLB, Bretenic Limited 810 Logan Avenue, Toronto, Ontario, Canada, M4K 3E1 Phone 416 466 8781 Fax 416 466 7190 paul@bretenic.ca**

I won my 5th grade spelling bee. Needless to say, I was on top of the world and looking to solidify my spot as king of the schoolyard. But somehow, somewhere, things went wrong. Very wrong. To this day, I can still hear the kids chanting "Punctuation Paul! Punctuation Paul!" over and over and over again. And the laughing. Oh how they laughed. Admittedly, the headgear and viola didn't help. But little did they know that prestige and glamour would come my way as a writer specializing in marketing and corporate communications. Rubbing shoulders with lawyers, accountants and HR professionals. You know, living the good life. Who's laughing now, Olivia Gillespie of homeroom 5C? Paul Russell, BA LLB Bretenic Limited, 810 Logan Avenue, Toronto, Ontario, Canada, M4K 3E1 Phone 416 466 8781 Fax 416 466 7190 paul@bretenic.ca

YOU

Bretenic Limited, 810 Logan Avenue, Toronto, Ontario, Canada, M4K 3E1

1 DESIGN FIRM
Tomko Design
ART DIRECTOR
Mike Tomko
DESIGNER
Mike Tomko
CLIENT
Six

2 DESIGN FIRM
Sussner Design
Company
ART DIRECTOR
Derek Sussner
DESIGNER
Bill Burns
CLIENT
Way North Films

3 DESIGN FIRM
Bob's Haus
DESIGNER
Bob Dahlquist
CLIENT
Tom Colicchio

4 DESIGN FIRM
Alexis Godefroy
ART DIRECTOR
Alexis Godefroy
DESIGNER
Alexis Godefroy
CLIENT
Cubik

5 DESIGN FIRM
Niedermeier Design
ART DIRECTOR
Kurt Niedermeier
DESIGNER
Kurt Niedermeier
CLIENT
Turfplus, Inc.

6 DESIGN FIRM
Compass360 Design
+ Advertising
ART DIRECTORS
John Cook
Karl Thomson
DESIGNER
Mark Buchner
CLIENT
Elevate

MINT

1

WAY NORTH FILMS

2

'wichcraft

3

CUBIK

4

TURFPLUS

5

ELEVATE

6

DESIGN FIRM
Elephant In The Room
ART DIRECTOR
Andy Trantham
DESIGNER
Robert Milam
CLIENT
Contempo
Furniture Store

DESIGN FIRM
LG2 Boutique
ART DIRECTORS
Serge Côte
Claude Auchu
DESIGNER
Serge Côte
CLIENT
LG2, LG2 Boutique,
LG2 Fabrique

DESIGN FIRM
LOWERCASE, INC.
ART DIRECTOR
Tim Bruce
DESIGNER
Tim Bruce
CLIENT
Map Lab

MAPLAB, INC. 4753 N. BROADWAY, SUITE 821, CHICAGO, IL 60640
T 773 989-8132 F 773 989-8133 WWW.MAPLAB.COM

MAPLAB, INC. 4753 N. BROADWAY, SUITE 821, CHICAGO, IL 60640
T 773 989-8132 F 773 989-8133 WWW.MAPLAB.COM

RALPH HOFFMAN, PRINCIPAL

MAPLAB, INC. 4753 N. BROADWAY, SUITE 821, CHICAGO, IL 60640
T 773 989-8132 F 773 989-8133 RALPH@MAPLAB.COM

1 DESIGN FIRM
Design by Paskal
ART DIRECTOR
Petr Skala
DESIGNERS
Petr Skala
Lukáš Veverka
CLIENT
Design Center of
the Czech Republic

2 DESIGN FIRM
A3 Design
ART DIRECTOR
Alan Altman
DESIGNER
Amanda Altman
CLIENT
Urban Architectural
Group

3 DESIGN FIRM
Isotope 221
ART DIRECTOR
Christopher Cannon
DESIGNER
Christopher Cannon
CLIENT
Second Species

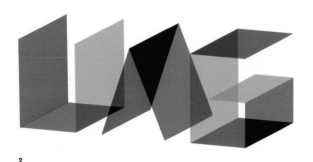

design
1

2

2ND SPECIES
3

DESIGN FIRM
3group
ART DIRECTORS
Ryszard Bienert
Sławomir Łukuc
DESIGNERS
Ryszard Bienert
Sławomir Łukuc
CLIENT
Group-Arch

DESIGN FIRM
Liska + Associates
ART DIRECTOR
Steve Liska
DESIGNER
Steve Liska
CLIENT
Contemporaine

CON
TEMP
ORAINE

DESIGN FIRM
Design Army
ART DIRECTORS
Pum Lefebure
Jake Lefebure
CLIENT
Karla Colletto
Swimwear

DESIGN FIRM
Korn Design
ART DIRECTORS
Denise Korn
Javier Cortes
DESIGNER
Ben Whitla
CLIENT
Champalimaud

CHAMPALIMAUD

CHAMPALIMAUD

CHAMPALIMAUD

Craig Mitchell
PROJECT DESIGNER

DIRECT 646.747.6524 FAX 646.328.3218
EMAIL craigm@champalimauddesign.com

One Union Square West, Suite 705, New York, NY 10003
P 212.807.8869 F 212.807.1742 champalimauddesign.com

One Union Square West, Suite 705, New York, NY 10003   P 212.807.8869   F 212.807.1742   champalimauddesign.com

DESIGN FIRM
Blok Design
ART DIRECTOR
Vanessa Eckstein
DESIGNERS
Vanessa Eckstein
Mariana Contegni
Patricia Kleeberg
CLIENT
Ödün

PLEASE ANSWER THE QUESTION.
WHAT'S YOUR FAVORITE SONG?
A. THE SOUND OF MUSIC
B. SINGING IN THE RAIN
C. BYE BYE BYE
D. NONE OF ABOVE
DO NOT CONTACT US AGAIN IF YOU ANSWER A TO C

Q101   01 : EMMIS   02 : WKQX-FM   03 : T 773 862 56 67
              BROADCASTING   MERCHANDISE   F 773 862 1214
              CORPORATION   MART PLAZA, STE. 1700
                                  CHICAGO, IL 60654

PLEASE ANSWER THIS QUESTION.
WHO'S YOUR FAVORITE SINGER?
A. RICKY MARTIN
B. BRITNEY SPEARS
C. ELVIS PRESLEY
D. NONE OF ABOVE
RETURN THIS CARD AND DO NOT CONTACT US AGAIN
IF YOU ANSWER A TO C.

CATHIE ANEST
PRODUCTION COORDINATOR
01:   EMMIS   02:   WKQX-FM   03: T 773 862 5667
      BROADCASTING   MERCHANDISE   F 773 862 1214
      CORPORATION   MART PLAZA, STE. 1700
                         CHICAGO, IL 60654
Q101

PLEASE ANSWER THIS QUESTION.
WHAT'S YOUR FAVORITE RADIO STATION?
A. Q101
B. 108FM
C. 94.4FM
D. 103.5FM

DO NOT CONTACT US AGAIN IF YOU ANSWER B TO D

Q101   01 : EMMIS   02 : WKQX-FM   03 : T 773 862 56 67
              BROADCASTING   MERCHANDISE   F 773 862 1214
              CORPORATION   MART PLAZA, STE. 1700
                                  CHICAGO, IL 60654

DESIGN FIRM
Korn Design
ART DIRECTORS
Denise Korn
Javier Cortes
DESIGNER
Sarah Daley
CLIENT
Steuben's Restaurant

DESIGN FIRM
LG2 Boutique

ART DIRECTORS
Sophie Lyonnais
Claude Auchu

DESIGNER
Sophie Lyonnais

CLIENT
Morency Société
D'Avocats

DESIGN FIRM
Bunch

ART DIRECTOR
Bunch

DESIGNER
Bunch

CLIENT
Vanja Solin
Proces 15

DESIGN FIRM
Zync Communications, Inc.
CREATIVE DIRECTOR
Marko Zonta
ART DIRECTOR
Mike Kasperski
DESIGNER
Mike Kasperski
Peter Wong
CLIENT
Blue Bamboo Yoga

DESIGN FIRM
Bernstein-Rein
Advertising

DESIGNER
Nathaniel Cooper

CLIENT
Paul Lerner
+ Associates

PAUL LERNER **&** ASSOCIATES
P.O. BOX 11124
SHAWNEE MISSION, KS 66207
T. 913 649 0457   F. 913 649 2070
PLERNERASSOCIATES.COM

PAUL LERNER
PRESIDENT & FOUNDER

PL **&** A
FUNDRAISING & EVENTS

P.O. BOX 11124
SHAWNEE MISSION, KS 66207
PLERNERASSOCIATES.COM

PAUL LERNER **&** ASSOCIATES

PL **&** A
FUNDRAISING & EVENTS

SELF-CONTAINED

DESIGN FIRM
Tim Frame Design
ART DIRECTOR
Grace Kim
DESIGNER
Tim Frame
CLIENT
REAL SIMPLE
Magazine

DESIGN FIRM
Tim Frame Design
ART DIRECTOR
Tim Frame
DESIGNER
Tim Frame
CLIENT
Billy's Bakery

1 DESIGN FIRM
FUNNEL: Eric Kass

DESIGNER
Eric Kass

CLIENT
Linnea's Lights

2 DESIGN FIRM
FUNNEL: Eric Kass

DESIGNER
Eric Kass

CLIENT
Saarinen Artist Reps

3 DESIGN FIRM
FUNNEL: Eric Kass

DESIGNER
Eric Kass

CLIENT
Punam Bean
Photography

1

2

3

Lg **LAYLA GRAYCE** *2004*
LOVE YOUR LIFE, EXPRESS YOUR STYLE
TRADE MARK

LAYLA GRAYCE

145 N. Sierra Madre Blvd | Suite 9 | Pasadena, CA 91107

Lg **LAYLA GRAYCE** *2004*
LOVE YOUR LIFE, EXPRESS YOUR STYLE
TRADE MARK

LAYLA GRAYCE
Wendy Estes | wendy@laylagrayce.com
145 N. Sierra Madre Blvd | Suite 9 | Pasadena, CA 91107
626.356.2133 | 626.356.2179
LAYLAGRAYCE.COM

STEVE BERG

est. 1981

BUILDING AND DESIGN

One Huntley Road
Richmond, VA 23226

P: 804.353.3444
F: 804.353.3321

STEVE BERG

BUILDING AND DESIGN

One Huntley Road, Richmond, Virginia 23226
P: 804.353.3444 | F: 804.353.3321

fold

fold

When you see it, you know it. The small details and little touches that make one thing stand out from the rest. Sometimes it's hard to pinpoint or even describe what makes something unique. It can be subtle and difficult to articulate. But if you keep your eyes open and really look, you can find it. And you'll know it when you see it.

Building and Design are my profession. My customers are my business. Every cut, every nail and every job must be done to a standard set by two authorities. One is the professional pride of a craftsman. The other is the satisfaction of the customer. One standard. Two authorities: my profession and my business.

One Huntley Road, Richmond, Virginia 23226
P: 804.353.3444 | C: 804.357.5120 | F: 804.353.3321
Steve@BergBuilding.com | www.BergBuilding.com

Communication is the key. Our customers communicate their needs to us. We depend on that communication to guide the process that leads to what we ultimately design and build. Then, when the work is complete, something new and interesting is communicated about the owner,

1 DESIGN FIRM
christiansen : creative
ART DIRECTOR
Tricia Christiansen
DESIGNER
Tricia Christiansen
CLIENT
St. Croix
Souvenir Co.

2 DESIGN FIRM
Wink
ART DIRECTOR
Scott Thares
DESIGNER
Scott Thares
CLIENT
Winston's

3 DESIGN FIRM
Timber Design Co.
ART DIRECTOR
Lars Lawson
DESIGNER
Lars Lawson
CLIENT
American Art
Clay Company

4 DESIGN FIRM
TOKY
Branding + Design
ART DIRECTOR
Eric Thoelke
DESIGNER
Travis Brown
CLIENT
100 Wood
Fire Grille

5 DESIGN FIRM
William Homan
Design
ART DIRECTOR
William Homan
DESIGNER
William Homan
CLIENT
West Yellowstone
Fly Shop

6 DESIGN FIRM
Cognetix
ART DIRECTOR
Tim Hogan
DESIGNER
Tim Hogan
CLIENT
Asten Johnson

1

2

3

4

5

6

DESIGN FIRM
Pavone, Inc.

ART DIRECTOR
Robinson C. Smith

DESIGNER
Nicole Gable

CLIENT
Clark Resources

DESIGN FIRM
Element
ART DIRECTOR
John McCollum
DESIGNERS
Jeremy Slagle
Meg Russell
CLIENT
Element

DESIGN FIRM
Sussner
Design Company
ART DIRECTOR
Derek Sussner
DESIGNER
Jamie Paul
CLIENT
Pardon My French
Bakery, Café and
Wine Bar

701 East Bay Street, Suite 6100  Charleston, South Carolina 29403

Julie A. Jensen
Sales Manager

701 E. Bay Street, Suite 6100
Charleston, SC 29403
T | 843.577.3600 C | 843.810.3682
Julie@CigarFactoryCharleston.com

701 East Bay Street, Suite 6100 | Charleston, SC 29403 | CigarFactoryCharleston.com

DESIGN FIRM
Lolight Design
ART DIRECTOR
Aaron Deckler
DESIGNER
Aaron Deckler
CLIENT
TSC
Travel Support Center

DESIGN FIRM
FUNNEL: Eric Kass
DESIGNER
Eric Kass
CLIENT
Ed McCulloch
Photography

1 DESIGN FIRM
Niedermeier Design
ART DIRECTOR
Kurt Niedermeier
DESIGNER
Kurt Niedermeier
CLIENT
Red Rocket Press

2 DESIGN FIRM
Behaviour /
Cadson Demak
ART DIRECTORS
Pongtorn Hiranpruek
Anuthin Wongsunkakon
DESIGNER
Pongtorn Hiranpruek
Anuthin Wongsunkakon
Noraphon Uktanan
CLIENT
Sea Munch
Seafood Galleria

3 DESIGN FIRM
Tim Frame Design
ART DIRECTOR
Melissa Hasebrook
DESIGNER
Tim Frame
CLIENT
Upper Arlington
High School

4 DESIGN FIRM
The Jones Group
ART DIRECTOR
Vicky Jones
DESIGNER
Jason Ottinger
CLIENT
29 Cosmetics

5 DESIGN FIRM
Studio Output
ART DIRECTOR
Rob Coke
DESIGNER
Stewart McMillan
CLIENT
Brik Barbershop

6 DESIGN FIRM
Entermotion
Design Studio
DESIGNER
Lea Morrow
CLIENT
Scooper Joe's

3

1

2

4

6

5

DESIGN FIRM
die Transformer
ART DIRECTORS
Martin Schonhoff
Michael Theile
DESIGNERS
Martin Schonhoff
Michael Theile
CLIENT
ProjektFabrik

Projektfabrik e.V. · Ruhrtal 5 · 58456 Witten

PROJEKTFABRIK E.V.
Ruhrtal 5
58456 Witten
Telefon: 02302/2035230
Fax: 02302/2035229
www.projektfabrik.org
kontakt@projektfabrik.org

SANDRA SCHÜRMANN
Geschäftsführung

PROJEKTFABRIK E.V.
Ruhrtal 5 · 58456 Witten
Telefon: 02302/2035230
Fax: 02302/2035229
www.projektfabrik.org
schuermann@projektfabrik.org

★ **GESCHÄFTSFÜHRUNG**
Sandra Schürmann
Simon Rieser

BANKVERBINDUNG
Volksbank Bochum Witten
BLZ 43060129
Konto 627034300

DESIGN FIRM
Wink
ART DIRECTORS
Richard Boynton
Scott Thares
DESIGNER
Richard Boynton
CLIENT
Cine-O-Matic

712 ONTARIO AVE. W. MINNEAPOLIS, MN 55403
TELEPHONE: 612/236-9160 FACSIMILE: 612/236-9161
WWW.CINEOMATICMEDIA.COM

HD-MEDIA   A DIVISION OF Copycats® MEDIA INCORPORATED

BRIAN DEHLER
BRIAN.DEHLER@CINEOMATICMEDIA.COM

712 ONTARIO AVE. W. MINNEAPOLIS, MN 55403
TELEPHONE: 612/236-9160 FACSIMILE: 612/236-9161
WWW.CINEOMATICMEDIA.COM

HD-MEDIA   A DIVISION OF Copycats® MEDIA INCORPORATED

712 ONTARIO AVE. W. MINNEAPOLIS, MN 55403
TELEPHONE: 612/236-9160 FACSIMILE: 612/236-9161
WWW.CINEOMATICMEDIA.COM

HD-MEDIA   A DIVISION OF Copycats® MEDIA INCORPORATED

DESIGN FIRM
Tim Frame Design
ART DIRECTOR
Tim Frame
DESIGNER
Tim Frame
CLIENT
The Dennis Miller
Show

KNOWLEDGE OF WEALTH ‖ **TDC** ‖ WEALTH OF KNOWLEDGE

ST. LOUIS SM

Bradley J. Delp, ChFC
Cleves R. Delp, ChFC
Christopher E. Erblich
David S. Sherman, III

Houston, Texas
Maumee, Ohio
Phoenix, Arizona
Southern California

TDC ST. LOUIS

PAIGE BREWER
EXECUTIVE ADMINISTRATOR

190 Carondelet Plaza, Suite 1450 St. Louis, MO 63105
P: 314-880-9999 F: 314-880-9997
E: pbrewer@tdcstl.com www.tdcstl.com

Securities offered through LPL Financial Member FINRA/SIPC

KNOWLEDGE OF WEALTH ‖ WEALTH OF KNOWLEDGE

ST. LOUIS SM

190 Carondelet Plaza, Suite 1450
St. Louis, MO 63105

190 Carondelet Plaza, Suite 1450 St. Louis, MO 63105 P: 314-880-9999 F: 314-880-9997 www.tdcstl.com

Securities offered through LPL Financial Member FINRA/SIPC

DESIGN FIRM
Annabelle Fiset
ART DIRECTOR
Annabelle Fiset
DESIGNER
Annabelle Fiset
CLIENT
Annabelle Fiset

DESIGN FIRM
Hybrid Design
ART DIRECTOR
Brian Flynn
DESIGNER
Caleb Kozlowski
CLIENT
Super 7

DESIGN FIRM
WORK Labs
ART DIRECTOR
Cabell Harris
DESIGNER
Paul Howalt
CLIENT
WORK Labs

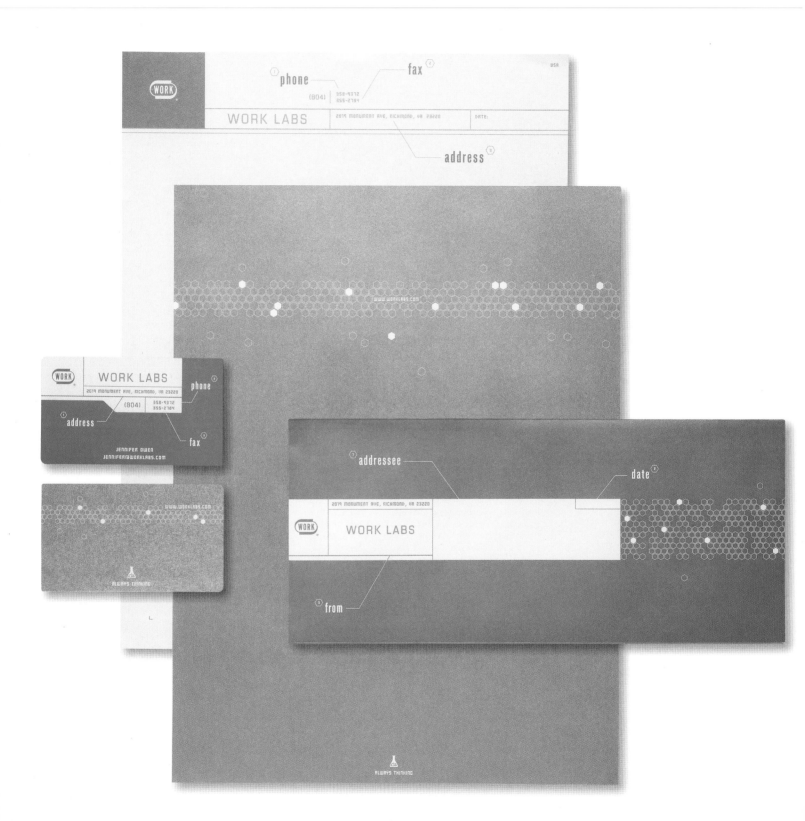

DESIGN FIRM
Passing Notes
DESIGNER
Abbie Planas Gong
CLIENT
Isabelle's Table

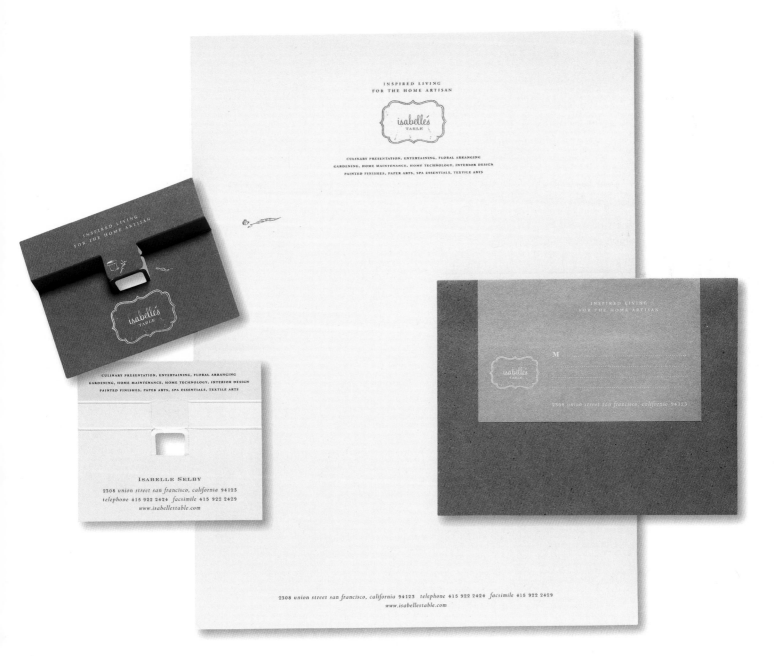

1 DESIGN FIRM
Kuhlmann
Leavitt, Inc.
ART DIRECTOR
Deanna
Kuhlmann-Leavitt
DESIGNER
Tom Twellmann
CLIENT
B+T Pizza

2 DESIGN FIRM
S Design, Inc.
ART DIRECTOR
Cara Sanders Robb
DESIGNER
Jesse Davison
CLIENT
Schlegel Bicycles

3 DESIGN FIRM
Tim Frame Design
ART DIRECTOR
Paul Howalt
DESIGNER
Tim Frame
CLIENT
1241

4 DESIGN FIRM
Zync
Communications, Inc.
ART DIRECTORS
Marko Zonta
Mike Kasperski
DESIGNER
Mike Kasperski
CLIENT
Weston Forest
Group

5 DESIGN FIRM
Transistor Design
ART DIRECTOR
Maxime Rheault
DESIGNER
Maxime Rheault
CLIENT
Antenne-A

6 DESIGN FIRM
Default
ART DIRECTORS
Anisa Suthayalai
Alex Lin
DESIGNERS
Anisa Suthayalai
Alex Lin
CLIENT
Gargyle

1

2

3

4

5

6

DESIGN FIRM
Hook
ART DIRECTOR
Brady Waggoner
DESIGNER
Brady Waggoner
CLIENT
Folbot

Parade Organics
235B Cambie Street
Vancouver, BC Canada V6B 5A4

info@parade.ca

We are Always Organic™ 🐦

Parade Organics
235B Cambie Street, Vancouver BC V6B 5A4
TEL 604.687.7163 FAX 604.687.7113 www.parade.ca

DESIGN FIRM
Wink

ART DIRECTOR
Scott Thares

DESIGNER
Scott Thares

CLIENT
MTV

DESIGN FIRM
Rethink
CREATIVE DIRECTORS
Ian Grais
Chris Staples
DESIGNER
Jeff Harrison
CLIENT
Kolachy Co.

DESIGN FIRM
¡Hola Chorizo!

ART DIRECTOR
Jorge Lamora

DESIGNER
Jorge Lamora

CLIENT
Masterpiece
Delicatessen

1 DESIGN FIRM
Sussner
Design Company
ART DIRECTOR
Derek Sussner
DESIGNER
Brandon Van Liere
CLIENT
Moneycenter

2 DESIGN FIRM
Hook
ART DIRECTOR
Brady Waggoner
DESIGNER
Brady Waggoner
CLIENT
Sucker Jeans

3 DESIGN FIRM
Design Sense
ART DIRECTOR
Katelyne De Muelenaere
DESIGNER
Katelyne De Muelenaere
CLIENT
Frederik De Clercq

1

2

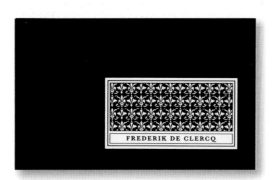

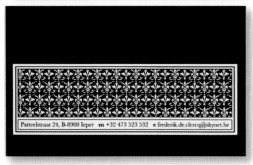

3

DESIGN FIRM
ID Branding
DESIGNER
Jared Milam
CLIENT
ID Branding

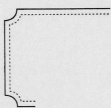

IDBRANDING.COM

TEL
503 223 7737

fax 503 223 2719
520 SOUTHWEST YAMHILL STREET, SUITE 800
PORTLAND, OR 97204

branding

IDBRANDING.COM

TEL
503 223 7737

fax 503 223 2719
520 SOUTHWEST YAMHILL STREET, SUITE 800
PORTLAND, OR 97204

MARC HEWITT

Interactive Producer
march@idbranding.com

direct 503 548 6343

IDBRANDING.COM

520 SOUTHWEST YAMHILL STREET, SUITE 800
PORTLAND, OR 97204

branding

ICONIC

DESIGN FIRM
Design Army

ART DIRECTORS
Pum Lefebure
Jake Lefebure

DESIGNER
Tim Madle

CLIENT
Virginia Film Festival:
Aliens!

DESIGN FIRM
die Transformer
ART DIRECTORS
Martin Schonhoff
Michael Theile
DESIGNERS
Martin Schonhoff
Michael Theile
CLIENT
die Transformer

1 DESIGN FIRM
Wink

ART DIRECTORS
Richard Boynton
Scott Thares

DESIGNER
Richard Boynton

CLIENT
Mayo Woodlands

2 DESIGN FIRM
Luke Despatie
& The Design Firm

ART DIRECTOR
Luke Despatie

DESIGNER
Luke Despatie

CLIENT
The North Side

3 DESIGN FIRM
Murillo Design, Inc.

ART DIRECTOR
Rolando G. Murillo

DESIGNER
Rolando G. Murillo

CLIENT
Sean Claes

4 DESIGN FIRM
Elephant In The Room

ART DIRECTOR
Andy Trantham

DESIGNER
Andy Trantham

CLIENT
Specialty Retail
Development Co.

1

2

3

4

1 DESIGN FIRM
Murillo Design, Inc.
ART DIRECTOR
Stan McElrath
DESIGNER
Rolando G. Murillo
CLIENT
Atlas Culinary
Adventures

2 DESIGN FIRM
Catapult
Strategic Design
ART DIRECTOR
Art Lofgreen
DESIGNER
Art Lofgreen
CLIENT
Zwick Construction
Company

3 DESIGN FIRM
Markatos \ Moore
ART DIRECTOR
Tyler Moore
DESIGNER
Peter Markatos
CLIENT
Disfigure

4 DESIGN FIRM
Behaviour /
Cadson Demak
ART DIRECTOR
Pongtorn Hiranpruek
DESIGNER
Pongtorn Hiranpruek
CLIENT
Roti.com (Restaurant)

1

2

3

4

DESIGN FIRM
LG2 Boutique
ART DIRECTORS
Cindy Goulet
Claude Auchu
DESIGNER
Cindy Goulet
CLIENT
topreservation.ca

1 DESIGN FIRM
Catapult
Strategic Design
ART DIRECTOR
Art Lofgreen
DESIGNER
Art Lofgreen
CLIENT
Universal
Technical Institute

2 DESIGN FIRM
Diseño Dos Asociados
ART DIRECTORS
Juan Carlos Garcia
Carlos Rivera
DESIGNER
Juan Carlos Garcia
CLIENT
Ross Centro Llantero

3 DESIGN FIRM
Greteman Group
ART DIRECTOR
Sonia Greteman
DESIGNER
Chris Parks
CLIENT
Kansas Aviation
Museum

4 DESIGN FIRM
Greteman Group
ART DIRECTOR
Sonia Greteman
DESIGNER
Chris Parks
CLIENT
FlightSafety
International

5 DESIGN FIRM
Hotiron Creative, LLC
DESIGNER
Melanie Warner
CLIENT
Hotiron Creative

6 DESIGN FIRM
Murillo Design, Inc.
ART DIRECTOR
Rolando G. Murillo
DESIGNER
Rolando G. Murillo
CLIENT
Mindspace

1

2

3

4

5

6

1 DESIGN FIRM
Lewis
Communications
ART DIRECTOR
Robert Froedge
DESIGNER
Robert Froedge
CLIENT
Advantage
Home Inspection

2 DESIGN FIRM
Extract Associated
Designers
ART DIRECTOR
Daniel Fabian
DESIGNER
Thomas Iwainsky
CLIENT
Immoangola LDA

3 DESIGN FIRM
Entermotion
Design Studio
ART DIRECTOR
Lea Morrow
DESIGNER
Lea Morrow
CLIENT
Paste

4 DESIGN FIRM
UNIT-Y
ART DIRECTOR
Andrey Nagomy
DESIGNER
Andrey Nagomy
CLIENT
International
Truck Company

5 DESIGN FIRM
Sommese Design
ART DIRECTOR
Lanny Sommese
DESIGNER
Lanny Sommese
CLIENT
Greg Copenhaver,
Realtor

6 DESIGN FIRM
One Zero Charlie
ART DIRECTORS
Michael Stanard
DESIGNER
Mary Errin
CLIENT
Atlas Brush Company

1

2

3

4

5

6

DESIGN FIRM
Design Army

ART DIRECTORS
Pum Lefebure
Jake Lefebure

DESIGNER
Lucas Badger

CLIENT
Miiko Salon

DESIGN FIRM
Lam Design Group
ART DIRECTOR
Linda T. Lam
DESIGNER
Linda T. Lam
CLIENT
The Wine Tie

1 DESIGN FIRM
Rickabaugh Graphics

ART DIRECTOR
Eric Rickabaugh

DESIGNER
Nathan Orensten

CLIENT
Big East Conference

2 DESIGN FIRM
Rickabaugh Graphics

ART DIRECTOR
Eric Rickabaugh

DESIGNER
Chris Franklin

CLIENT
UCSB Sand Sharks

3 DESIGN FIRM
Tim Frame Design

ART DIRECTOR
Tim Frame

DESIGNER
Tim Frame

CLIENT
touristees.com

4 DESIGN FIRM
The Bradford Lawton
Design Group

CREATIVE DIRECTOR
Bradford Lawton

DESIGNER
Lisa Kaltman

CLIENT
Frontier Enterprises

5 DESIGN FIRM
Rickabaugh Graphics

ART DIRECTOR
Eric Rickabaugh

DESIGNER
Eric Rickabaugh

CLIENT
Duquesne Dukes

6 DESIGN FIRM
Steven Dreyer Design

ART DIRECTOR
Steven Dreyer

DESIGNER
Steven Dreyer

CLIENT
Yard Boy Landscaping

1

2

3

4

5

6

DESIGN FIRM
Kevin Akers
design + imagery
ART DIRECTOR
Kevin Akers
DESIGNER
Kevin Akers
CLIENT
Judee + Kevin's
Wedding Icons

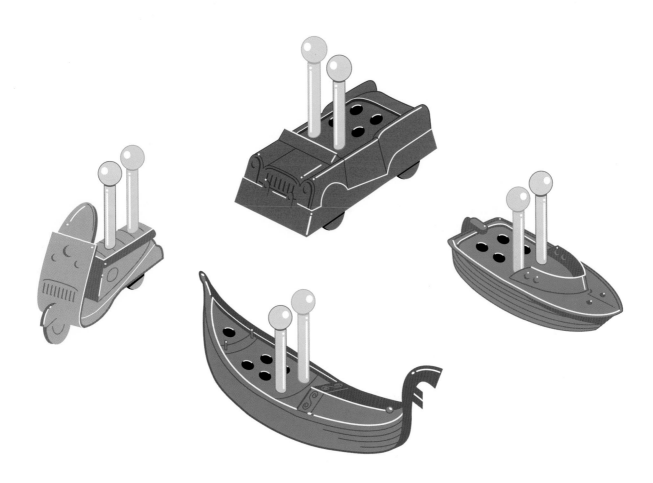

1 DESIGN FIRM
Mirko Ilic Corp.

ART DIRECTOR
Mirko Ilic

DESIGNER
Mirko Ilic

CLIENT
Paradoxy
Products

2 DESIGN FIRM
Oxide Design Co.

DESIGNER
Drew Davies
Joe Sparano

CLIENT
Saddle Creek
Records

3 DESIGN FIRM
Miriello Grafico

DESIGNER
Dennis Garcia

CLIENT
The Children's
Initiative Group

1

SL●WDOWN

2

3

PICTURES

19 EAST 16TH STREET APT 4F NEW YORK, NY 10003
WWW.MANSIONPICTURESNY.COM

HANNAH DAVIS 917 674 9703
HANNAH@MANSIONPICTURESNY.COM
WWW.MANSIONPICTURESNY.COM

mansion
PICTURES

mansion
PICTURES   19 EAST 16TH ST APT 4F NEW YORK, NY 10003

WWW.MANSIONPICTURESNY.COM

1 DESIGN FIRM
Design Army
ART DIRECTORS
Pum Lefebure
Jake Lefebure
DESIGNER
Tim Madle
CLIENT
Signature Theatre

2 DESIGN FIRM
Design Army
ART DIRECTORS
Pum Lefebure
Jake Lefebure
DESIGNER
Tim Madle
CLIENT
Wal-Mart Watch

3 DESIGN FIRM
The General
Design Company
DESIGNERS
Soung Wiser
Scott Livingston
CLIENT
Ross G. Bates
Consulting

4 DESIGN FIRM
Kevin Akers
design + imagery
ART DIRECTOR
Kevin Akers
DESIGNER
Kevin Akers
CLIENT
Grenada Tours /
Travel

1

2

3

4

1 DESIGN FIRM
SK Designworks
ART DIRECTOR
Soonduk Krebs
DESIGNER
Jason Kernevich
CLIENT
Free Air Time
Campaign

2 DESIGN FIRM
Rethink
CREATIVE DIRECTORS
Ian Grais
Chris Staples
DESIGNER
Jeff Harrison
CLIENT
The Canadian Press

FREE ★ AIR ★ TIME
CAMPAIGN
WWW.FREEAIRTIME.ORG

1

THE CANADIAN PRESS

2

DESIGN FIRM
Okan Usta

ART DIRECTOR
Okan Usta

DESIGNER
Okan Usta

CLIENT
Kerem Kurdoglu

1 DESIGN FIRM
RANGE

ART DIRECTOR
John Swieter

DESIGNER
Garrett Owen

CLIENT
Dialogic

2 DESIGN FIRM
Murillo Design, Inc.

ART DIRECTOR
Rolando G. Murillo

DESIGNER
Rolando G. Murillo

CLIENT
The Living Room
Recording Studio

3 DESIGN FIRM
Pink Blue Black
& Orange Co., Ltd.

ART DIRECTOR
Vichean Tow

DESIGNER
Wansawad Chantien

CLIENT
Ketvadi – Gadini

4 DESIGN FIRM
Murillo Design, Inc.

ART DIRECTOR
Rolando G. Murillo

DESIGNER
Kim Arispe

CLIENT
Phase Fire
Management

5 DESIGN FIRM
Steve's Portfolio

DESIGNER
Steve De Cusatis

CLIENT
JEG

6 DESIGN FIRM
Bernstein-Rein
Advertising

DESIGNER
Nathaniel Cooper

CLIENT
Bottle Rocket

1

2

3

4

5

6

DESIGN FIRM
Design Ranch
ART DIRECTORS
Michelle Sonderegger
Ingred Sidie
DESIGNER
Tad Carpenter
CLIENT
chefBURGER

DESIGN FIRM
Compass360 Design
+ Advertising

ART DIRECTORS
John Cook
Karl Thomson

DESIGNER
John Cook
Kelly Ferguson

CLIENT
Stokefire

STOKEFIRE

IGNITING BRANDS
Dana FitzGerald
Client Experience Consultant
dana@stokefire.com

7001 Loisdale Road, Suite C,
Springfield, VA 22150
TollFree: 866-STOKEFIRE
Phone: 703-778-9925

1 DESIGN FIRM
Pumpkinfish

DESIGNER
Jon Berg

CLIENT
Pumpkinfish

2 DESIGN FIRM
Isaac Arthur

ART DIRECTOR
Isaac Arthur

DESIGNER
Isaac Arthur

CLIENT
Dave Skully

1

SKULLY'S
GUN CLUB

2

DESIGN FIRM
Pentagram Design
ART DIRECTOR
DJ Stout
DESIGNER
Daniella Boebel
CLIENT
Emerald City Press

Pentagram Design
Daniella Boebel

DESIGN FIRM
Design Army
ART DIRECTOR
Pum Lefebure
Jake Lefebure
DESIGNER
Tim Madle
CLIENT
AIGA DC: Show Off

DESIGN FIRM
Wink

ART DIRECTOR
Scott Thares

DESIGNER
Scott Thares

CLIENT
Cooper-Hewitt
Museum

DESIGN FIRM
Wink

ART DIRECTORS
Richard Boynton
Scott Thares

DESIGNER
Richard Boynton

CLIENT
Mayo Woodlands

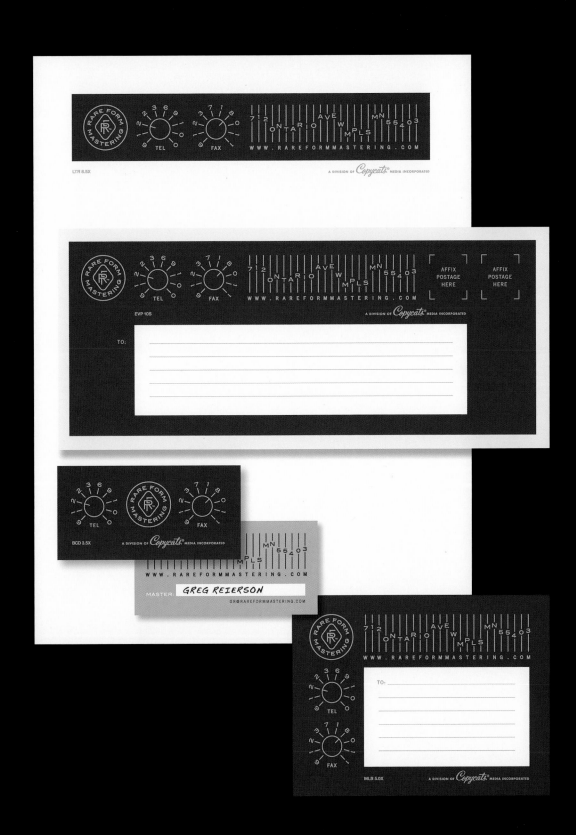

1 DESIGN FIRM
Ryan Smoker
Design
DESIGNER
Ryan Smoker
CLIENT
Crossway Church

2 DESIGN FIRM
3 Advertising
DESIGNER
Tim McGrath
CLIENT
Mojo Associates

3 DESIGN FIRM
Lam Design Group
ART DIRECTOR
Linda T. Lam
DESIGNER
Linda T. Lam
CLIENT
The Windy Hill
Tree Farm

4 DESIGN FIRM
REACTOR
ART DIRECTOR
Clifton Alexander
DESIGNER
Heather Grice
CLIENT
Modus Propane

1

2

3

4

DESIGN FIRM
Ogilvy & Mather
ART DIRECTOR
David Eller
DESIGNER
David Eller
CLIENT
Lenovo
Carolina Hopefest

DESIGN FIRM
Kevin Akers
design + imagery
ART DIRECTOR
Kevin Akers
DESIGNER
Kevin Akers
CLIENT
Benefit Growth Fund

1 DESIGN FIRM
Go Welsh

ART DIRECTOR
Craig Welsh

DESIGNER
Nichelle Narcisi

CLIENT
Royer's Flowers
& Gifts

2 DESIGN FIRM
The General
Design Company

DESIGNERS
Soung Wiser
Scott Livingston

CLIENT
Green the Air

3 DESIGN FIRM
KBDA

ART DIRECTOR
Kim Baer

DESIGNERS
Liz Burrill
Allison Bloss

CLIENT
Wildwood School

4 DESIGN FIRM
LG2 Boutique

ART DIRECTORS
Julie Bisson
Claude Auchu

DESIGNER
Julie Bisson

CLIENT
Maison Du
Développment
Durable

1

2

3

4

DESIGN FIRM
Design Army
ART DIRECTORS
Pum Lefebure
Jake Lefebure
DESIGNER
Tim Madle
CLIENT
Virginia Film Festival:
Kinflicks

1 DESIGN FIRM
M-Art

ART DIRECTOR
Marty Ittner

CLIENT
Pyramid Atlantic
Art Center

2 DESIGN FIRM
Hook

ART DIRECTOR
Jason Johnson

DESIGNER
Brady Waggoner

CLIENT
Stone Soup

3 DESIGN FIRM
The Heads of State

ART DIRECTORS
Jason Kernevich
Dustin Summers

DESIGNER
Jason Kernevich

CLIENT
Quills

4 DESIGN FIRM
Rome & Gold Creative

ART DIRECTOR
Lorenzo Romero

DESIGNER
Carlos Bobadilla

CLIENT
Coffee Mystica

1

2

3

4

1 DESIGN FIRM
Steve's Portfolio
DESIGNER
Steve De Cusatis
CLIENT
JEG

2 DESIGN FIRM
Rubin Cordaro
Design
ART DIRECTOR
Bruce Rubin
DESIGNER
Jim Cordaro
CLIENT
The Overfors Group

3 DESIGN FIRM
LG2 Boutique
ART DIRECTORS
Serge Cóte
Claude Auchu
DESIGNER
Serge Cóte
CLIENT
Foundation de Etoiles

4 DESIGN FIRM
Scientific Arts
DESIGNER
Quan Xuan
CLIENT
Vic Watch Security

1

2

3

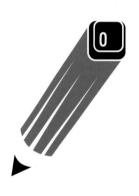

4

1 DESIGN FIRM
Pentagram Design
ART DIRECTOR
DJ Stout
DESIGNER
Daniella Boebel
CLIENT
Blum Brands

2 DESIGN FIRM
Fresh Oil
ART DIRECTOR
Dan Stebbings
DESIGNER
Dan Stebbings
CLIENT
Rhode Runner

3 DESIGN FIRM
Tomko Design
ART DIRECTOR
Mike Tomko
DESIGNER
Mike Tomko
CLIENT
School Supply Store

4 DESIGN FIRM
Fresh Oil
ART DIRECTOR
Dan Stebbings
DESIGNER
Dan Stebbings
CLIENT
Fresh Oil

5 DESIGN FIRM
Bruketa & Zinic OM
ART DIRECTOR
Tomislav Jurica
Kacunic
DESIGNER
Tomislav Jurica
Kacunic
CLIENT
Agency for Science
and Higher Education
Croatia

6 DESIGN FIRM
The Jones Group
ART DIRECTOR
Vicky Jones
DESIGNER
Kendra Lively
CLIENT
Cenitare
Restaurant Group

1

2

3

4

5

6

DESIGN FIRM
Willoughby
Design Group
ART DIRECTORS
Ann Willoughby
Nate Hardin
DESIGNERS
Nate Hardin
Jessica McEntire
CLIENT
Kevin Carroll

HANDCRAFTED

DESIGN FIRM
Ryan Russell Design

ART DIRECTOR
Ryan Russell

DESIGNER
Ryan Russell

CLIENT
Students Against
Genocide in Africa
(SAGA)

DESIGN FIRM
Struck

ART DIRECTOR
Peder Singleton

DESIGNER
Dan Christofferson

CLIENT
Vast

DESIGN FIRM
The Creative Method
ART DIRECTOR
Tony Ibbotson
DESIGNER
Andi Yanto
CLIENT
Sue Arthur
(Over the Moon Dairy Co.)

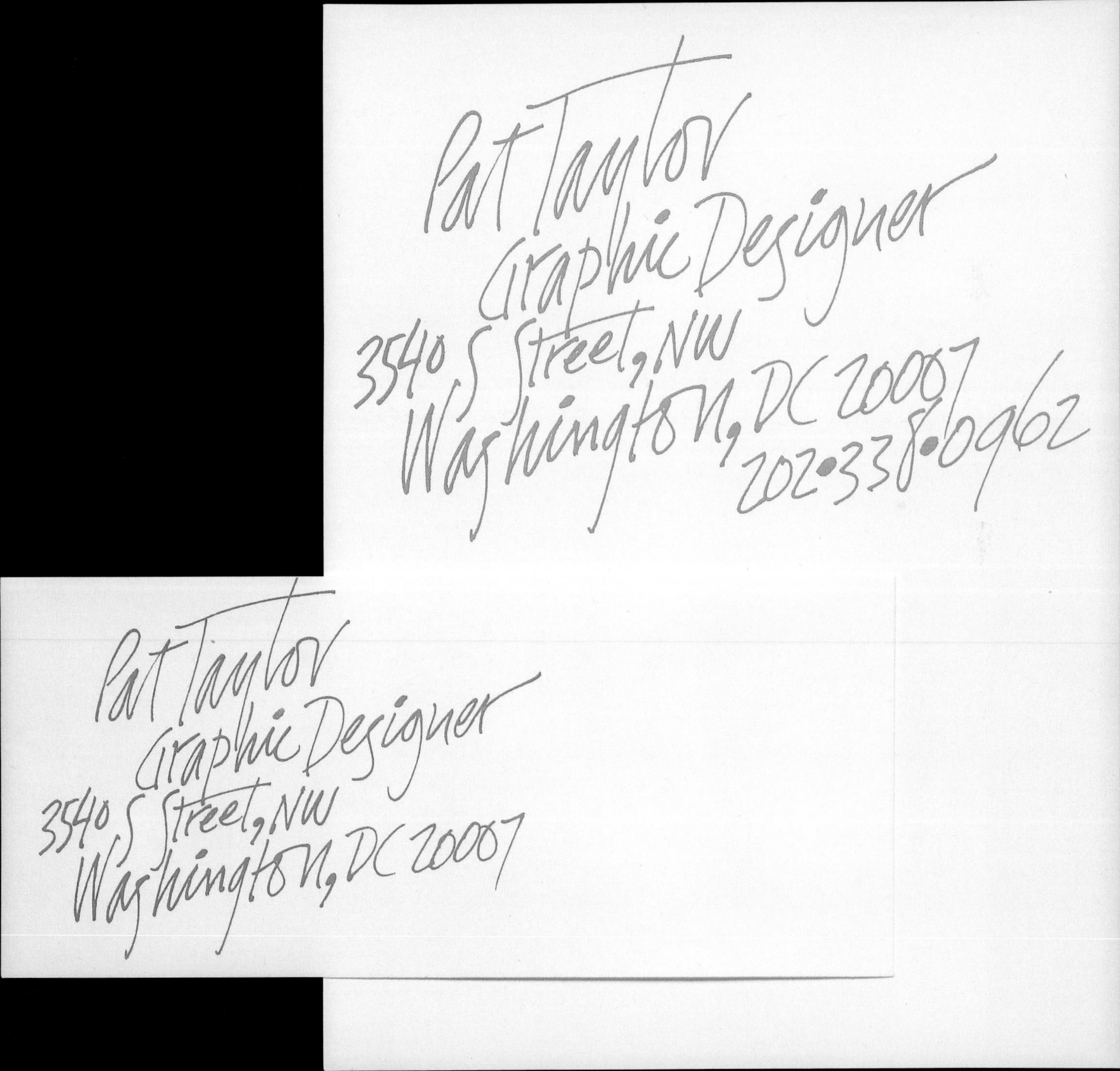

Pat Taylor
Graphic Designer
3540 S Street, NW
Washington, DC 20007
202•338•0962

Pat Taylor
Graphic Designer
3540 S Street, NW
Washington, DC 20007

first vine wine imports + sales 1642 argonne pl, nw washington dc 20009

first vine wine imports + sales 1642 argonne pl, nw washington dc 20009
t 202 744 9597 f 866 381 6010 first.vine@verizon.net www.firstvine.com

tom natan, partner

first vine wine imports + sales 1642 argonne pl, nw washington dc 20009 t 202 744 9597 f 866 381 6010 www.firstvine.com

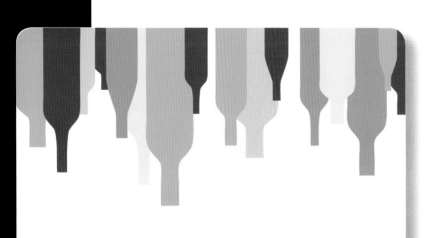

1 DESIGN FIRM
Go Welsh

ART DIRECTOR
Craig Welsh

DESIGNER
Nichelle Narcisi

CLIENT
Music For Everyone

2 DESIGN FIRM
Studio Output

DESIGNER
Sam Campbell

CLIENT
Loosefilms

1

2

DESIGN FIRM
Passing Notes
DESIGNER
Abbie Planas Gong
CLIENT
Peek…aren't
you curious

DESIGN FIRM
Tilka Design
ART DIRECTOR
Jane Tilka
DESIGNERS
Shannon Busse
Katrin Ioss
CLIENT
MB Artists

DESIGN FIRM
Passing Notes
DESIGNER
Abbie Planas Gong
CLIENT
Passing Notes

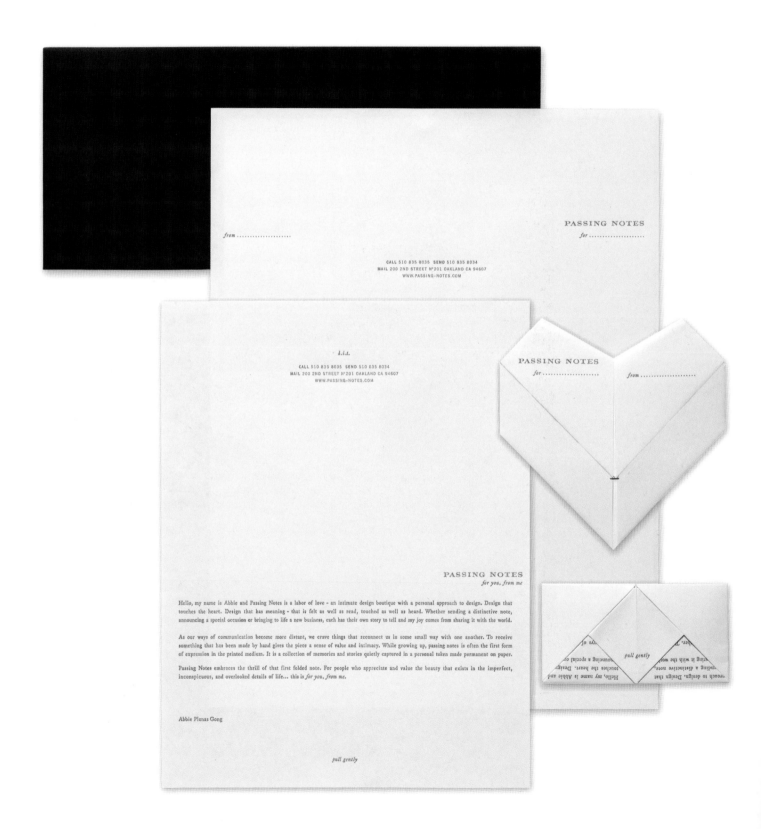

1 DESIGN FIRM
TOKY
Branding + Design

ART DIRECTOR
Eric Thoelke

DESIGNER
Travis Brown

CLIENT
David Eicholtz

2 DESIGN FIRM
Synergy Graphix

ART DIRECTOR
Remo Strada

DESIGNER
Remo Strada

CLIENT
New York
Trail Runners

1

2

1 DESIGN FIRM
TOKY
Branding + Design
ART DIRECTOR
Eric Thoelke
DESIGNER
Travis Brown
CLIENT
Art the Vote

2 DESIGN FIRM
Alphabet Arm Design
ART DIRECTOR
Aaron Belyea
DESIGNER
Ryan Frease
CLIENT
Proof Wine Marketing

1

2

pink blue black & orange co., ltd. (color party)
1128 rama 9 road, suanluang, bangkok 10250 thailand
tel. (662) 300 5124, fax. (662) 300 5123
mailus@colorparty.com, color_party@hotmail.com
www.colorparty.com
an associate of **The Design Alliance**™ a collaborative network
of asian design consultancies

punlarp punnotok
design director

perund sethabutra
graphic designer

suhaila madeeyoah
administrator

pink blue black & orange co., ltd. (color party)
1128 rama 9 road, suanluang, bangkok 10250 thailand
tel. (662) 300 5124, fax. (662) 300 5123
mailus@colorparty.com, color_party@hotmail.com
www.colorparty.com
an associate of **The Design Alliance**™ a collaborative network
of asian design consultancies

pink blue black & orange co., ltd. (color party)
1128 rama 9 road, suanluang, bangkok 10250 thailand
tel. (662) 300 5124, fax. (662) 300 5123
mailus@colorparty.com, color_party@hotmail.com
www.colorparty.com
an associate of **The Design Alliance**™ a collaborative network
of asian design consultancies

DESIGN FIRM
Korn Design
ART DIRECTORS
Denise Korn
Javier Cortes
DESIGNERS
Melissa Wehrman
Ben Whitla
CLIENT
Sage Restaurant
Group

DESIGN FIRM
Chen Design
Associates

ART DIRECTORS
Joshua C. Chen
Laurie Carrigan

DESIGNER
Max Spector

CLIENT
Yoshi's Jazz Club &
Japanese Restaurant

DESIGN FIRM
Smog Design, Inc.
ART DIRECTOR
Sara Cummings
DESIGNER
Sara Cummings
CLIENT
Dangerbird Records

IMPULSE

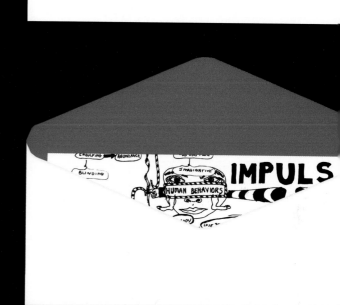

IMPULSE

August 22, 2008

Nunc interdum
694 Aptent Lane
New York, NY 10013

Dear Lorem Ipsum,

Lorem ipsum dolor sit amet, consectetuer adipiscing elit. Sed tellus sapien, malesuada interdum, pulvinar quis, malesuada quis, leo. Pellentesque pede nunc, laoreet in, convallis eget, mollis eget, ante. Pellentesque felis sapien, pretium sed, tristique quis, iaculis eu, dolor. Proin sit amet eros quis massa condimentum condimentum. Donec nec nibh id lectus pellentesque luctus. Nam tincidunt, augue vitae placerat pretium, purus neque aliquam nibh, ut tristique mauris ligula ac purus. Donec velit. Donec faucibus tincidunt erat. Sed vestibulum, nisl sed dignissim tincidunt, ipsum nisi semper turpis, non ullamcorper sapien metus vel purus. Vivamus metus pede, ornare nec, pretium nec, elementum a, felis.

Ut eu odio. Morbi posuere nisi et purus. Integer fermentum velit id dui. Phasellus et turpis eget erat dignissim dapibus. Phasellus hendrerit risus. Aliquam non nunc at felis commodo gravida. Sed fringilla. Etiam dapibus, diam laoreet lobortis feugiat, risus justo tempor enim, consectetuer sodales nulla tortor in neque. Fusce nibh urna, scelerisque quis, faucibus id, imperdiet in, lorem. Duis sollicitudin fermentum nibh. Vestibulum porttitor condimentum sem.

Etiam viverra luctus nisl. Integer accumsan, purus non facilisis tempor, arcu orci blandit ipsum, non pharetra mi justo a turpis. Cras elementum. Proin at turpis. Integer at mi. Aenean erat. Curabitur ipsum. Vivamus neque. Phasellus tincidunt blandit orci. In pulvinar. Praesent augue neque, sollicitudin a, dictum ornare, laoreet a, elit. Duis viverra, leo ac blandit volutpat, tellus ipsum consequat leo, ac rhoncus tortor velit at erat. Donec tortor est, convallis a, gravida non, molestie in, ante. Nulla facilisi. Pellentesque habitant morbi tristique senectus et netus et malesuada fames ac turpis egestas. Fusce condimentum blandit urna. Maecenas diam sapien, consequat a, sagittis eu, placerat eleifend, enim. Aliquam lobortis turpis.

Sincerely,
Lobortis Turpis

335 Greenwich Street, Suite 7A
New York, NY 10013

www.impulsefeatures.com

8100 BOONE BLVD, STE 120
VIENNA, VIRGINIA 22182
TELEPHONE 703 891 7888
FACSIMILE 703 891 7886
YOUTHFILMACADEMY.COM

YOUTH
FILM
ACADEMY

8100 BOONE BLVD, STE 120
VIENNA, VIRGINIA 22182
TELEPHONE 703 891 7888
FACSIMILE 703 891 7886
YOUTHFILMACADEMY.COM

YOUTH
FILM
ACADEMY

D, STE 120
NIA 22182
3 891 7888
3 891 7886
DEMY.COM

TH
M
MY

YOUTH
FILM
ACADEMY

1 DESIGN FIRM
Nocturnal Graphic
Design Studio

ART DIRECTOR
Ken Peters

DESIGNER
Ken Peters

CLIENT
Fox Restaurant
Concepts

2 DESIGN FIRM
Unconstruct

ART DIRECTOR
Victor Aguilar

DESIGNER
Victor Aguilar

CLIENT
canvasface.com
Ashley May

1

2

1 DESIGN FIRM
Tilka Design
ART DIRECTOR
Jane Tilka
DESIGNERS
Shannon Busse
Susanne LeBlanc
CLIENT
Werc Werk Works

2 DESIGN FIRM
Pink Blue Black
& Orange Co., Ltd.
ART DIRECTOR
Vichean Tow
DESIGNER
Ratinun Thaijarurn
CLIENT
Chef Film

1

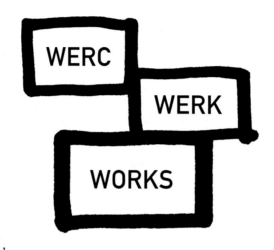

2

DESIGN FIRM
Neogine
Communication
Design

ART DIRECTOR
Campbell MacDuff

DESIGNERS
Jonathan Lord
Yasmine El Orfi
Nick De Jardine

CLIENT
New Zealand Film
and Television School

THE NEW ZEALAND FILM AND TELEVISION SCHOOL

filmschool.org.nz PO Box 27-044, Wellington 6141, New Zealand   T +64 4 939-2954   E info@filmschool.org.nz

DESIGN FIRM
Lizette Gecel
DESIGNER
Lizette Gecel
CLIENT
Lizette Gecel

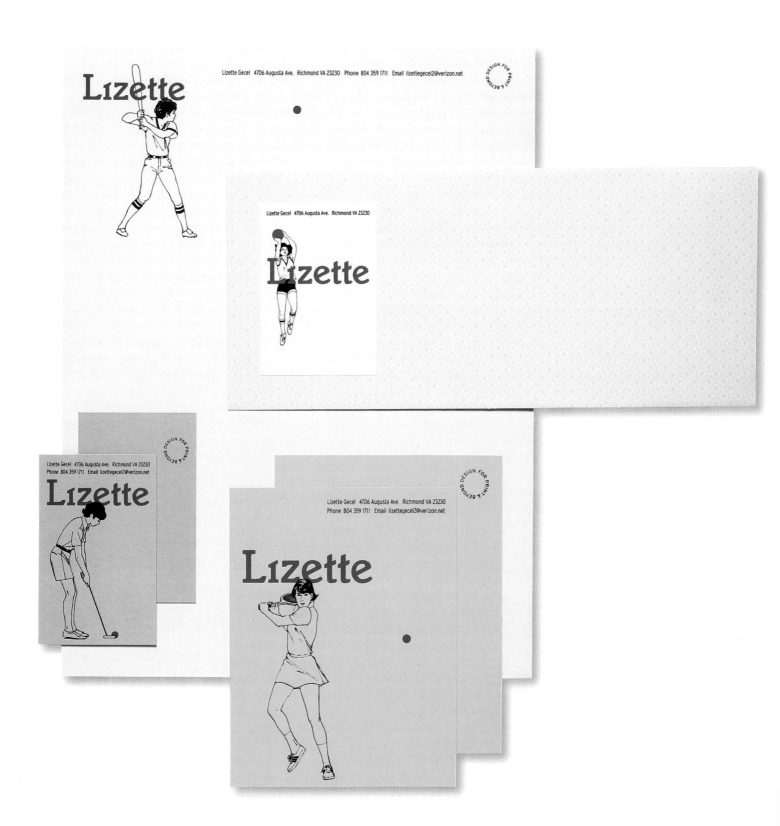

DESIGN FIRM
The Creative Method
ART DIRECTOR
Tony Ibbotson
DESIGNER
Tony Ibbotson
CLIENT
Sweet Dreams Cakes

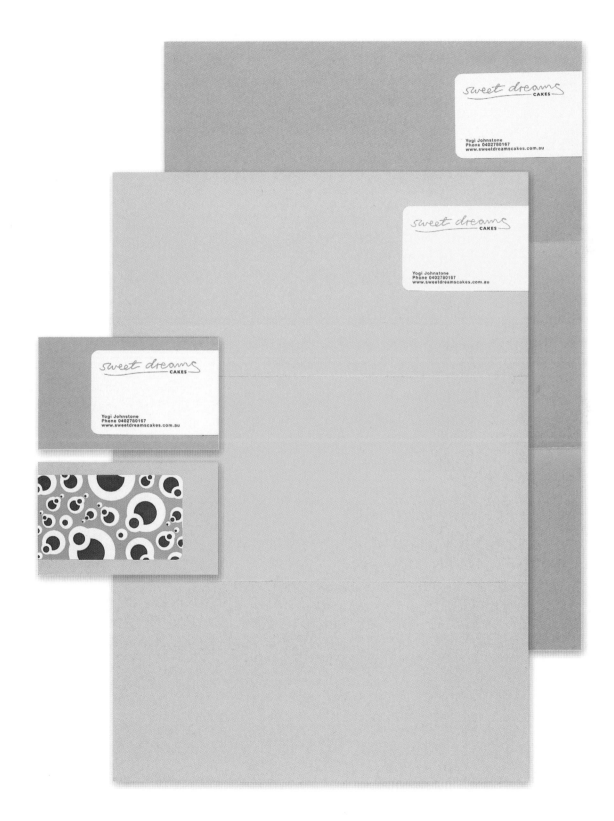

LETTERFORM

ART DIRECTOR
Petter Ringbom
DESIGNER
Dan Arbello
CLIENT
Redscout

REDSCOUT

28 West 25th Street
10th Floor
New York, NY 10010
T 646 336 6028
F 646 336 6122

REDSCOUT

1 DESIGN FIRM
People Design, Inc.

CREATIVE DIRECTOR
Geoffrey Mark

DESIGNER
Brian Hauch
Marie-Claire Camp
Jason Murray
Tim Calkins

CLIENT
Creative Byline

2 DESIGN FIRM
die Transformer

ART DIRECTORS
Martin Schonhoff
Michael Theile

DESIGNERS
Martin Schonhoff
Michael Theile

CLIENT
TU Dortmund
Transferstelle

3 DESIGN FIRM
Wink

ART DIRECTORS
Richard Boynton
Scott Thares

DESIGNER
Richard Boynton

CLIENT
Target

4 DESIGN FIRM
Slant, Inc.

ART DIRECTOR
Ryan Gagnard

DESIGNER
Ryan Gagnard

CLIENT
DataBank

1

2

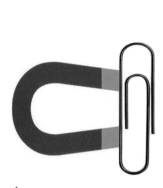

3

4

DESIGN FIRM
Pencil

ART DIRECTOR
Luke Manning

DESIGNER
Luke Manning

CLIENT
Rock & Road

1 DESIGN FIRM
The Bradford Lawton
Design Group
CREATIVE DIRECTOR
Bradford Lawton
DESIGNER
Bradford Lawton
CLIENT
Melody Hair Salon

2 DESIGN FIRM
Wink
ART DIRECTORS
Richard Boynton
Scott Thares
DESIGNER
Richard Boynton
CLIENT
Marshall Field's

3 DESIGN FIRM
Archrival
ART DIRECTOR
Joe Kreutzer
DESIGNER
Joe Kreutzer
CLIENT
W Hair Studio

4 DESIGN FIRM
Pink Blue Black
& Orange Co., Ltd.
ART DIRECTOR
Siam Attariya
DESIGNER
Siam Attariya
CLIENT
Hair Master

1

2

3

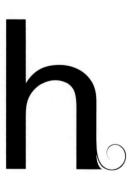

4

1 DESIGN FIRM
Design Army
ART DIRECTOR
Pum Lefebure
Jake Lefebure
DESIGNER
Tim Madle
CLIENT
World Security
Institute

2 DESIGN FIRM
Poulin + Morris, Inc.
DESIGNERS
Richard Poulin
Brian Brinaisi
AJ Mapes
CLIENT
LeFrak Organization

3 DESIGN FIRM
160 over 90
ART DIRECTORS
Darryl Cilli
Steve Penning
DESIGNER
Adam Flanagan
CLIENT
Scott Morrison
Maia Restaurant

4 DESIGN FIRM
Wink
ART DIRECTORS
Richard Boynton
Scott Thares
DESIGNER
Richard Boynton
CLIENT
Futureproof

5 DESIGN FIRM
Mirko Ilic Corp.
ART DIRECTOR
Mirko Ilic
DESIGNER
Mirko Ilic
CLIENT
Mirko Ilic Corp.

6 DESIGN FIRM
Alexander Egger
ART DIRECTOR
Alexander Egger
DESIGNER
Alexander Egger
CLIENT
Pilot Projekt

1

2

3

4

5

6

DESIGN FIRM
MINE

ART DIRECTOR
Christopher Simmons

DESIGNER
Tim Belonax

CLIENT
C+

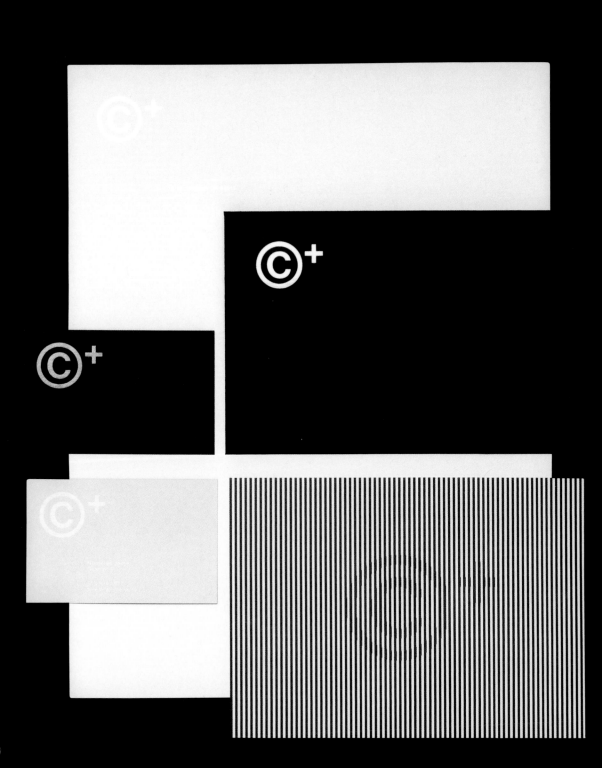

1 DESIGN FIRM
Design Army

ART DIRECTORS
Pum Lefebure
Jake Lefebure

DESIGNER
Tim Madle

CLIENT
Ask Dad

2 DESIGN FIRM
Hoet & Hoet

ART DIRECTOR
Nick Hoet

DESIGNER
Nick Hoet

CLIENT
Belsim SA

3 DESIGN FIRM
Design Army

ART DIRECTOR
Pum Lefebure
Jake Lefebure

DESIGNER
Sucha Becky

CLIENT
Roadside
Development

4 DESIGN FIRM
Rome & Gold
Creative

ART DIRECTOR
Lorenzo Romero

DESIGNER
Carlos Bobadilla

CLIENT
Integrity Designs

5 DESIGN FIRM
REACTOR

ART DIRECTOR
Clifton Alexander

DESIGNER
Chase Wilson

CLIENT
The Freelance
Exchange of
Kansas City

6 DESIGN FIRM
Catapult
Strategic Design

ART DIRECTOR
Art Lofgreen

DESIGNER
Art Lofgreen

CLIENT
Secure Data
Destruction

1

2

3

4

5

6

1 DESIGN FIRM
Rome & Gold
Creative
ART DIRECTOR
Robert E. Goldie
DESIGNER
Lorenzo Romero
CLIENT
Shepherd's School

2 DESIGN FIRM
Design Army
ART DIRECTORS
Pum Lefebure
Jake Lefebure
DESIGNER
Sucha Becky
CLIENT
Capitol
Communicator

3 DESIGN FIRM
Wink
ART DIRECTOR
Scott Thares
DESIGNER
Scott Thares
CLIENT
Girard Management

4 DESIGN FIRM
Lloyds Graphic
Design Ltd.
ART DIRECTOR
Alexander Lloyd
DESIGNER
Alexander Lloyd
CLIENT
Jigsaw Promotions

5 DESIGN FIRM
Doug Fuller, Logo
& Identity Designer
ART DIRECTOR
Doug Fuller
DESIGNER
Doug Fuller
CLIENT
Rivet

6 DESIGN FIRM
Bob Dinetz Design
ART DIRECTOR
Bob Dinetz
DESIGNER
Bob Dinetz
CLIENT
Shanghai Sales

1

2

3

4

5

6

1 DESIGN FIRM
Rome & Gold
Creative
ART DIRECTOR
Robert E. Goldie
DESIGNER
Lorenzo Romero
CLIENT
Shepherd's School

2 DESIGN FIRM
Design Army
ART DIRECTORS
Pum Lefebure
Jake Lefebure
DESIGNER
Sucha Becky
CLIENT
Capitol
Communicator

3 DESIGN FIRM
Wink
ART DIRECTOR
Scott Thares
DESIGNER
Scott Thares
CLIENT
Girard Management

4 DESIGN FIRM
Lloyds Graphic
Design Ltd.
ART DIRECTOR
Alexander Lloyd
DESIGNER
Alexander Lloyd
CLIENT
Jigsaw Promotions

5 DESIGN FIRM
Doug Fuller, Logo
& Identity Designer
ART DIRECTOR
Doug Fuller
DESIGNER
Doug Fuller
CLIENT
Rivet

6 DESIGN FIRM
Bob Dinetz Design
ART DIRECTOR
Bob Dinetz
DESIGNER
Bob Dinetz
CLIENT
Shanghai Sales

DESIGN FIRM
Compass360 Design
+ Advertising
ART DIRECTORS
Karl Thomson
John Cook
DESIGNER
Mark Buchner
CLIENT
CPM
Centres for Pain
Management

DESIGN FIRM
Pentagram Design
ART DIRECTOR
DJ Stout
DESIGNER
Daniella Boebel
CLIENT
ODIC Force Magazine

P.O. BOX 684729 AUSTIN, TX 78768-4729 P:512.535.3378 F:512.535.4844 C:512.626.6721

ODICFORCE MAGAZINE

JOHNSTON AYALA PUBLISHER, EDITORIAL DIRECTOR
ODICFORCEMAGAZINE.COM JOHN STON@ODICFORCEMAGAZINE.COM

ODICFORCE MAGAZINE

P.O.BO X68 4729A USTINTEXA S78 768-4729P:512.535.3 378F:512.535.4844WW W.ODICFORCEMAGAZINE.COM

1 DESIGN FIRM
RANGE

ART DIRECTOR
John Swieter

DESIGNERS
John Swieter
Garrett Owen

CLIENT
Banner Retail
Marketing

2 DESIGN FIRM
Catapult
Strategic Design

ART DIRECTOR
Art Lofgreen

DESIGNER
Art Lofgreen

CLIENT
Dr. Kelli Slate D.D.S.

3 DESIGN FIRM
Lewis
Communications

ART DIRECTOR
Robert Froedge

DESIGNER
Robert Froedge

CLIENT
Five Waters Resort

4 DESIGN FIRM
160 over 90

ART DIRECTORS
Darryl Cilli
Dan Shepelavy

DESIGNERS
Adam Flanagan
Adam Garcia

CLIENT
Woodmere
Art Museum

1

2

3

4

DESIGN FIRM
MSDS

ART DIRECTOR
Matthew Schwartz
Ryan Reynolds

DESIGNER
Nial O'Kelly

CLIENT
MetroSouth
Medical Center

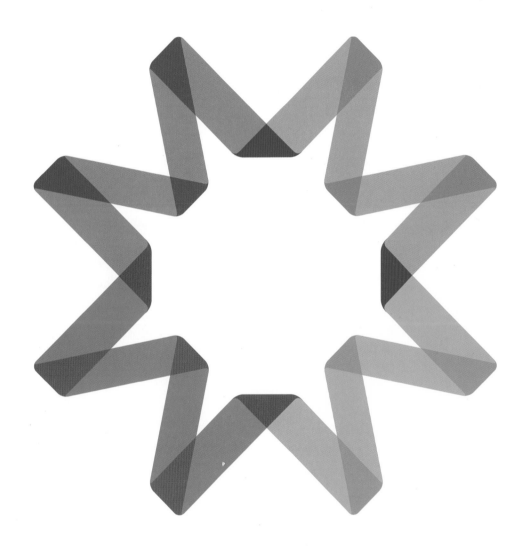

1 DESIGN FIRM
Steven Dreyer
Design
ART DIRECTOR
Steven Dreyer
DESIGNER
Steven Dreyer
CLIENT
Simply Play

2 DESIGN FIRM
3 Advertising
DESIGNER
Tim McGrath
CLIENT
Cliqs

3 DESIGN FIRM
PenguinCube
ART DIRECTOR
Tammam Yamout
DESIGNER
Lana Daher
CLIENT
Raio Paints

1

2

3

1 DESIGN FIRM
A3 Design

ART DIRECTOR
Alan Altman

DESIGNER
Amanda Altman

CLIENT
Wire Mesh
Office Supplies /
Carolina Pad & Paper

2 DESIGN FIRM
JJ Nelson Designs

ART DIRECTOR
Jeanette J. Nelson

DESIGNER
Jeanette J. Nelson

CLIENT
Heritage Recycling,
LLC

3 DESIGN FIRM
Slant, Inc.

ART DIRECTOR
Ryan Gagnard

DESIGNER
Ryan Gagnard

CLIENT
Jim Wilson
Architecture

4 DESIGN FIRM
Langton
Cherubino Group

ART DIRECTOR
David Langton

DESIGNER
Jim Keller

CLIENT
Renaissance
Capital, LLC

1

2

3

4

DESIGN FIRM
LG2 Boutique
ART DIRECTORS
Julie Bisson
Claude Auchu
DESIGNER
Julie Bisson
CLIENT
Stripes

1 DESIGN FIRM
Scientific Arts

DESIGNER
Quan Xuan

CLIENT
Majores Painters

2 DESIGN FIRM
Gramblin Design

ART DIRECTOR
David Gramblin

DESIGNER
David Gramblin

CLIENT
Allen Athletic
Consultants

3 DESIGN FIRM
id29

ART DIRECTOR
Doug Bartow

DESIGNER
Bryan Kahrs

CLIENT
Ryan-Biggs
Associates

4 DESIGN FIRM
Murillo Design, Inc.

ART DIRECTOR
Rolando G. Murillo

DESIGNER
Kim Arispe

CLIENT
KGB Texas

1

2

3

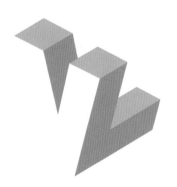

4

TIPPING
POINT
COMMUNITY

TIPPING
POINT
COMMUNITY

703 Market Street
Suite 708
San Francisco, CA
94103

o 415 348 1240
f 415 348 1237

tippoint.org

where good intentions become
tangible results

Rebecca Cherin
Director of Programs
rebecca@tippoint.org

linking resources to fight poverty

703 Market Street, Suite 708
San Francisco, CA 94103
o 415 348 1240 x302
f 415 348 1237

making poverty preventable, not inevitable

703 Market Street
Suite 708
San Francisco, CA
94103

o 415 348 1240
f 415 348 1237

tippoint.org

DESIGN FIRM
Spark Studio
ART DIRECTOR
Gary Domoney
DESIGNER
Gary Domoney
CLIENT
Architecture by
Russell Casper,
Architects

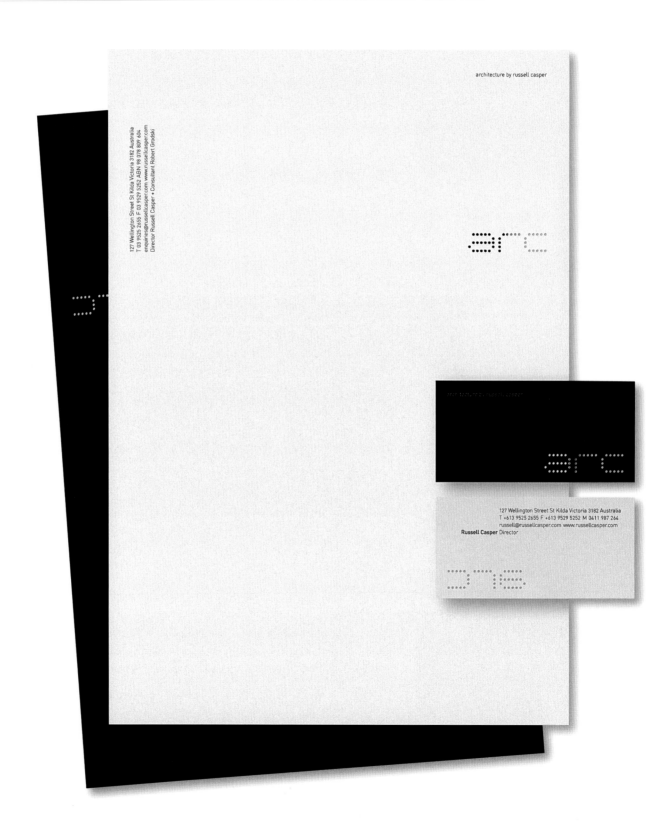

1 DESIGN FIRM
Mirko Ilic Corp.

ART DIRECTOR
Mirko Ilic

DESIGNER
Mirko Ilic

CLIENT
Djinjic Foundation

2 DESIGN FIRM
Stereotype Design

ART DIRECTOR
Mike Joyce

DESIGNER
Mike Joyce

CLIENT
Avenue A

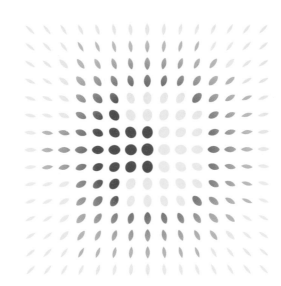

1

2

ABSTRACT

DESIGN FIRM
Default
ART DIRECTOR
L. Akarit
N. Sataporn
DESIGNER
L. Akarit
N. Sataporn
CLIENT
Ministry of Energy,
Thailand

1 DESIGN FIRM
Graphic Design
Studio by
Yurko Gutsulyak
ART DIRECTOR
Yurko Gutsulyak
DESIGNER
Yurko Gutsulyak
CLIENT
Helga Language
Learning Centre

2 DESIGN FIRM
Beth Singer
Design
ART DIRECTOR
Beth Singer
DESIGNER
Sucha Snidvongs
CLIENT
TCI

3 DESIGN FIRM
Gee + Chung
Design
ART DIRECTOR
Earl Gee
DESIGNER
Earl Gee
CLIENT
Off-Site Records
Management

4 DESIGN FIRM
3 Advertising
DESIGNER
Tim McGrath
CLIENT
Upaya

1

2

3

4

THE
NEW ZEALAND
CHEESE SCHOOL
LIMITED.

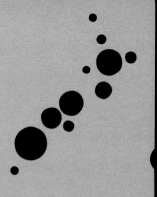

33 Tirau Street   P +64 7 8838 238   E office@newzealandcheeseschool.co.nz
Putaruru 3411   F +64 7 8838 235   www.newzealandcheeseschool.co.nz

**THE
NEW ZEALAND
CHEESE SCHOOL
LIMITED.**

Sue Arthur
Director

**THE
NEW ZEALAND
CHEESE SCHOOL
LIMITED.**

**THE
NEW ZEALAND
CHEESE SCHOOL
LIMITED.**

DESIGN FIRM
Pat Taylor
Graphic Design
ART DIRECTOR
Pat Taylor
DESIGNER
Pat Taylor
CLIENT
Almost Perfect

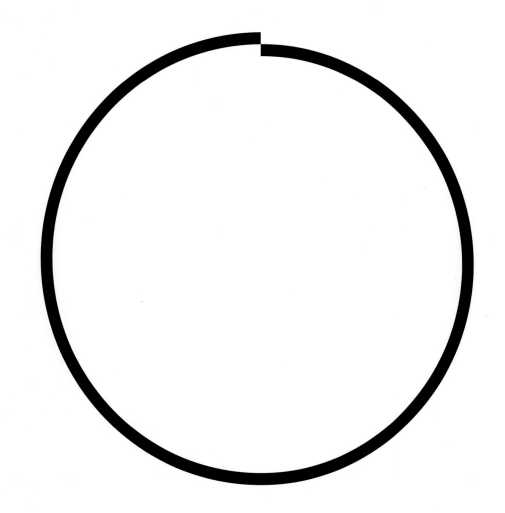

DESIGN FIRM
Element
ART DIRECTOR
John McCollum
DESIGNER
Meg Russell
CLIENT
Hypersight
Consulting, Inc.

DESIGN FIRM
Graphic Design Studio
by Yurko Gutsulyak
CREATIVE DIRECTOR
Yurko Gutsulyak
DESIGNER
Yurko Gutsulyak
CLIENT
Legal Consulting
Group, Ltd

   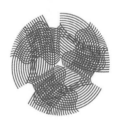

  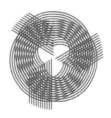 

DESIGN FIRM
Bunch

ART DIRECTOR
Bunch

DESIGNER
Bunch

CLIENT
Flores

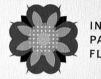 INSTITUT PARFUMEUR FLORES

 INSTITUT PARFUMEUR FLORES

ŽANETA RODIĆ
PRESIDENT
M +385 91 4811 850
E ZANETA@FLORES-GROUP.COM

FLORES GROUP
DOLAC 9
10000 ZAGREB / CROATIA
T +385 1 4828 287
F +385 1 4828 285
WWW.FLORES-GROUP.COM

 INSTITUT PARFUMEUR FLORES

 INSTITUT PARFUMEUR FLORES

 INSTITUT PARFUMEUR FLORES

 INSTITUT PARFUMEUR FLORES

 INSTITUT PARFUMEUR FLORES

 INSTITUT PARFUMEUR FLORES

DESIGN FIRM
BIZ-R

ART DIRECTOR
Blair Thomson

DESIGNERS
Tish England
Paul Warren

CLIENT
St. Mellion Flowers

a fresh foundation for florists

ST
**MELLION
FLOWERS.**

Rendar House
Woodacre Court
Saltash, Cornwall
PL12 6LF

T: 01752 845545
F: 01752 844309
E: info@stmellionflowers.co.uk
www.stmellionflowers.co.uk

Vat No: 418141867

DESIGN FIRM
Public, Inc.

ART DIRECTOR
Todd Foreman

DESIGNER
Tessa Lee

CLIENT
Public, Inc.

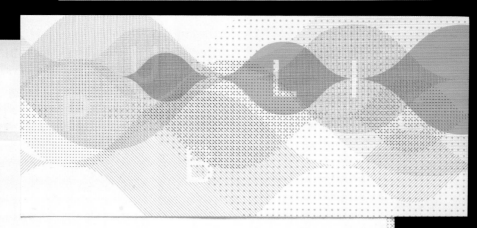

1 DESIGN FIRM
Chen Design
Associates
ART DIRECTORS
Joshua C. Chen
Laurie Carrigan
DESIGNER
Max Spector
CLIENT
Ecstasis
Consulting, LLC

2 DESIGN FIRM
Design Army
ART DIRECTOR
Pum Lefebure
DESIGNER
Sucha Becky
CLIENT
Golden Triangle

3 DESIGN FIRM
Compass360 Design
+ Advertising
ART DIRECTORS
John Cook
Karl Thomson
DESIGNER
Scott Wise
CLIENT
Possible Worlds

4 DESIGN FIRM
Chen Design
Associates
ART DIRECTOR
Joshua C. Chen
DESIGNER
Max Spector
CLIENT
Firefly Solar

5 DESIGN FIRM
Re-Generate
Design
ART DIRECTOR
Janet McBurney
DESIGNER
Janet McBurney
CLIENT
Stonehouse
Sound Inc.

6 DESIGN FIRM
Paragon Marketing
Communications
ART DIRECTOR
Lougi Alasfahani
DESIGNER
Huzaifa Kakumama
CLIENT
Beyout
Investment Group

1

2

3

4

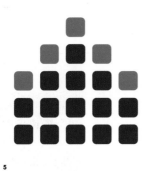

5

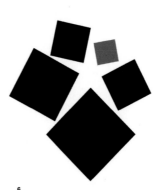

6

1 DESIGN FIRM
3 Advertising

DESIGNER
Tim McGrath

CLIENT
Medical Error
Reduction Program

2 DESIGN FIRM
Steve's Portfolio

DESIGNER
Steve De Cusatis

CLIENT
JEG

3 DESIGN FIRM
MSDS

ART DIRECTOR
Matthew Schwartz

DESIGNERS
Dan Sim
Ryan Reynolds

CLIENT
Trade, Aid and
Security Coalition
(TASC)

4 DESIGN FIRM
Mirko Ilić Corp.

ART DIRECTOR
Mirko Ilić

DESIGNER
Mirko Ilić

CLIENT
Memorial of
Nadezde Petrovic

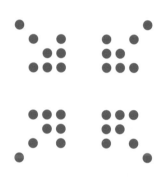

1

2

3

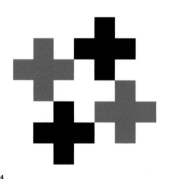

4

DESIGN FIRM
LG2 Boutique
ART DIRECTOR
Anne-Marie Clermont
DESIGNER
Anne-Marie Clermont
CLIENT
La Maison Théâtre

DESIGN FIRM
Bunch

ART DIRECTOR
Bunch

DESIGNER
Bunch

CLIENT
Rob Star
Star of Bethnal Green

∾ bette troy

T 508.380.5845

∾ bette troy

THIRTY FIVE OAK HILL ROAD, SOUTHBOROUGH, MA 01745
BETTE@BETTETROY.COM | WWW.BETTETROY.COM

THE ZOO

DESIGN FIRM
The Bradford Lawton
Design Group
ART DIRECTOR
Bradford Lawton
DESIGNER
Bradford Lawton
CLIENT
San Antonio
Zoo Ball '08

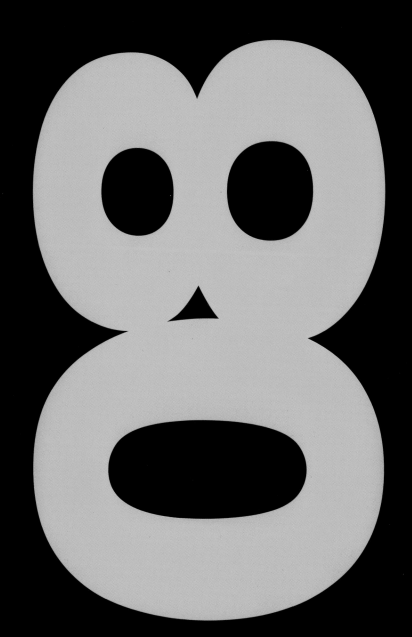

DESIGN FIRM
Sagmeister, Inc.
ART DIRECTOR
Stefan Sagmeister
DESIGNER
Richard The
CLIENT
Azuero Earth Project

AZUERO
EARTH
PROJECT

DESIGN FIRM
Carbone
Smolan Agency
ART DIRECTOR
Leslie Smolan
DESIGNER
Nina Masuda
CLIENT
Bideawee

bideawee®

bideawee®

DESIGN FIRM
Sussner
Design Company

ART DIRECTOR
Derek Sussner

DESIGNER
Brandon Van Liere

CLIENT
Animal Humane
Society

1 DESIGN FIRM
Qualia

ART DIRECTOR
David Hillel

DESIGNER
David Hillel

CLIENT
IGGY

2 DESIGN FIRM
Oxide Design Co.

DESIGNERS
Drew Davies
Joe Sparano
Craig Hughes
Chris Kelly

CLIENT
Firstar Fiber

3 DESIGN FIRM
Weber
Shandwick
Visual
Communications

ART DIRECTOR
Beth Pedersen

DESIGNER
Beth Pedersen

CLIENT
Dallas Zoological
Society

4 DESIGN FIRM
Smog Design, Inc.

ART DIRECTOR
Jeni Heiden

DESIGNER
Glen Nakasako

CLIENT
Dogpeople, Inc.

5 DESIGN FIRM
Lloyds Graphic
Design Ltd.

ART DIRECTOR
Alexander Lloyd

DESIGNER
Alexander Lloyd

CLIENT
Taimate Stud

6 DESIGN FIRM
Sommese Design

ART DIRECTOR
Lanny Sommese

DESIGNER
Lanny Sommese

CLIENT
Dante's Restaurants

1

2

3

4

5

6

DESIGN FIRM
Rodrigo Márquez
ART DIRECTOR
Rodrigo Márquez
DESIGNER
Rodrigo Márquez
CLIENT
Cuineta

DESIGN FIRM
Rubber Design
ART DIRECTORS
Jacquie Van Keuren
Will Yarbrough
DESIGNER
Ian Gordon
CLIENT
Perch

DESIGN FIRM
David Eller
ART DIRECTOR
David Eller
DESIGNER
David Eller
CLIENT
Wendy Yang
Photography

Wendy Yang
Photography

1 DESIGN FIRM
MSDS
ART DIRECTOR
Matthew Schwartz
DESIGNERS
Dan Sim
Ryan Reynolds
CLIENT
Proclivity Systems

2 DESIGN FIRM
UMS Design
Studio
ART DIRECTOR
Ulhas Moses
DESIGNER
Ulhas Moses
CLIENT
International
Learning Journeys

3 DESIGN FIRM
RANGE
ART DIRECTOR
John Swieter
DESIGNERS
John Swieter
CLIENT
Pegasus
Environmental
Design

4 DESIGN FIRM
MINE
ART DIRECTOR
Christopher Simmons
DESIGNERS
Kate Earhart
Christopher Simmons
CLIENT
San Francisco
Parks Trust

5 DESIGN FIRM
Turner Duckworth:
London &
San Francisco
ART DIRECTORS
David Turner
Bruce Duckworth
DESIGNER
Shawn Rosenberger
CLIENT
Oakville Grocery

6 DESIGN FIRM
The Bradford Lawton
Design Group
CREATIVE DIRECTOR
Bradford Lawton
DESIGNER
Jason Limon
CLIENT
Alamo Ranch

1

2

3

4

5

6

DESIGN FIRM
Wink
ART DIRECTOR
Scott Thares
DESIGNER
Scott Thares
CLIENT
Target

DESIGN FIRM
Gee + Chung Design
ART DIRECTOR
Earl Gee
DESIGNER
Earl Gee
CLIENT
DCM

DESIGN FIRM
Gee + Chung Design

DESIGN FIRM
Rubber Design
ART DIRECTORS
Jacquie Van Keuren
Will Yarbrough
DESIGNER
Ian Gordon
CLIENT
Peekadoodle
Kids Club

DESIGN FIRM
Sussner
Design Company

ART DIRECTOR
Derek Sussner

DESIGNER
Brandon Van Liere

CLIENT
Saint Barts

SAINT BART'S

19 WAYZATA

56 MINNESOTA

BULLDOGS

1 DESIGN FIRM
Rickabaugh
Graphics
ART DIRECTOR
Eric Rickabaugh
DESIGNER
Nathan Orensten
CLIENT
UTSA Roadrunners

2 DESIGN FIRM
Rickabaugh
Graphics
ART DIRECTOR
Eric Rickabaugh
DESIGNER
Dave Cap
CLIENT
Ball Hawg

3 DESIGN FIRM
Rickabaugh
Graphics
ART DIRECTOR
Eric Rickabaugh
DESIGNER
Nathan Orensten
CLIENT
LA Tech

4 DESIGN FIRM
Tim Frame
Design
ART DIRECTOR
Scott Sommers
DESIGNER
Tim Frame
CLIENT
Wolverine

5 DESIGN FIRM
Bob Dinetz
Design
ART DIRECTOR
Bob Dinetz
DESIGNER
Bob Dinetz
CLIENT
Shanghai Sales

6 DESIGN FIRM
Rickabaugh
Graphics
ART DIRECTOR
Eric Rickabaugh
DESIGNER
Chris Franklin
CLIENT
Black Dog Lacrosse

1

2

3

4

5

6

DESIGN FIRM
MDG
DESIGNER
Kris Greene
CLIENT
Coco Pet Products

DESIGN FIRM
Graphic Moxie, Inc.
DESIGNER
Bridgit Krentzer
CLIENT
Three Hounds Gallery

29 SOUTH FRONT STREET *Wilmington*, NC 28401 TELEPHONE *910 815 3330*   three hounds GALLERY   THREEHOUNDSGALLERY.COM

three hounds
GALLERY

29 SOUTH FRONT STREET *Wilmington*, NC 28401 THREEHOUNDSGALLERY.COM

KATE OSBORN

29 SOUTH FRONT STREET
Wilmington, NC 28401

TELEPHONE *910 815 3330*
MOBILE 910 228 9271

KATE@THREEHOUNDSGALLERY.COM
THREEHOUNDSGALLERY.COM

three hounds
GALLERY

1 DESIGN FIRM
D*LSH Design
ART DIRECTOR
Lucia Dinh
DESIGNER
Lucia Dinh
CLIENT
Vet Finder

2 DESIGN FIRM
FRESH Design
ART DIRECTOR
David Barron
DESIGNER
David Barron
CLIENT
Cranston Pet
Rehabilitation

3 DESIGN FIRM
Turner Duckworth:
London
ART DIRECTORS
David Turner
Bruce Duckworth
DESIGNERS
Shawn Rosenberger
David Turner
CLIENT
Method, Inc.

4 DESIGN FIRM
Jeff Fisher
LogoMotives
ART DIRECTOR
Jeff Fisher
DESIGNER
Jeff Fisher
CLIENT
Cat Adoption Team

1

2

3

4

1 DESIGN FIRM
D*LSH Design

2 DESIGN FIRM
FRESH Design

3 DESIGN FIRM
Turner Duckworth:
London

4 DESIGN FIRM
Jeff Fisher
LogoMotives

1 DESIGN FIRM
Greteman Group
ART DIRECTOR
Sonia Greteman
DESIGNER
Chris Parks
CLIENT
Spay & Neuter
Kansas

2 DESIGN FIRM
Carbone Smolan
Agency
ART DIRECTORS
Carla Miller
Leslie Smolan
DESIGNERS
Erin Hall
Melissa Laux
CLIENT
Nizuc

3 DESIGN FIRM
Liska + Associates
ART DIRECTOR
Steve Liska
DESIGNER
Katie Schweitzer
CLIENT
MyPetSpace.com,
LLC

4 DESIGN FIRM
Vaughn Wedeen
Creative
ART DIRECTOR
Pamela Chang
DESIGNER
Pamela Chang
CLIENT
Animal Humane
Association

1

2

3

4

AMMA
MATERNITY

P.O. Box 16686
St. Louis Park, MN 55416

AMMA
MATERNITY

P.O. Box 16686
St. Louis Park, MN 55416

Sara Pearce
RN CNM

sara@ammamaternity.com
ammamaternity.com

(952) 926-BABY

DESIGN FIRM
Nocturnal Graphic
Design Studio

ART DIRECTOR
Ken Peters

DESIGNER
Ken Peters

CLIENT
Café Development
Company

DESIGN FIRM
Walsh Associates
ART DIRECTOR
Kerry Walsh
DESIGNER
David Gramblin
CLIENT
Dovetail Rabbit

DESIGN FIRM
Luke Despatie
& The Design Firm
ART DIRECTOR
Luke Despatie
DESIGNER
Luke Despatie
CLIENT
The International
Wild Bird Foundation

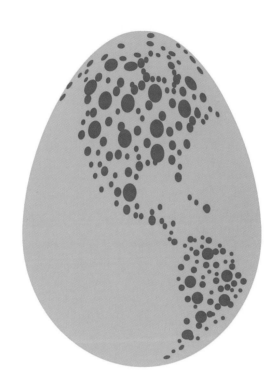

THE INTERNATIONAL WILD BIRD FOUNDATION

DIRECTORY

COMPASS360 DESIGN + ADVERTISING
11 Davies Avenue, Suite 200
Toronto, ON M4M 2A9
Canada
416.465.2299
www.compass360.com
47, 118, 168, 195

CONGNETIX
1866 Wallenberg Boulevard
Suite B
Charleston, SC 29407
USA
843.225.5558
www.cognetixllc.com
71, 217

THE CREATIVE METHOD
Studio 10, 50 Resevoir Street
Surry Hills, NSW 2010
Australia
+61 2.8231.9977
www.thecreativemethod.com
138, 157, 186

D*LSH DESIGN
16084 Carleton Street
Fountain Valley, CA 92708
USA
714.809.1106
www.dlshdesign.com
226

DAVID ELLER
400 North Church Street
Suite 615
Charlotte, NC 28202
USA
704.564.8900
www.creativehotlist.com/d-eller2
211

DEFAULT
64 E. 4th Street, 4th Floor
New York, NY 10003
USA
212.673.3160
www.defaultwebsite.info
17, 20, 33, 88, 192

DEFAULT (BANGKOK)
33 RJ D AND C Lock 5-6
Payathai, Bangkok
Thailand
602.270.1544
www.defaultbkk.org
58, 184

DENIZ MARLALI
47 Belair Road
Staten Island, NY 10305
USA
347.698.5773
www.denizmarlali.net
20

DESIGN ARMY
510 H Street NE
Washington, DC 20001
USA
202.797.1018
www.designarmy.com
42, 43, 54, 98, 106, 112, 121, 129,
140, 152, 164, 166, 167, 195

DESIGN BY PASKAL
Vlárská 12
Brno 627 00
Czech Republic
+420 602.573.103
www.designbypasakal.com
51

DESIGN RANCH
1600 Summit Street
Kansas City, MO 64108
USA
816.472.8668
www.design-ranch.com
21, 116—117

DESIGN SENSE
Patteelstraat 24
Ieper (Ypres) 8900
Belgium
+32 57.447.605
www.designsense.be
94

DISEÑO DOS ASOCIADOS
Vía Atlixcáyotl 5208
Torre JV1, Piso 9
San Andrés Cholula Puebla, 72830
Mexico
+52 222.431.0110
www.disenodos.com
104

DOTZERO DESIGN
208 SW Stark Street, #507
Portland, OR 97204
USA
503.892.9262
www.dotzerodesign.com
213

**DOUG FULLER
LOGO & IDENTITY DESIGNER**
2038 Durand Drive
Reston, VA 20191
USA
703.463.0450
www.dfdesigner.blogspot.com
33, 167

ELEMENT
3757 North High Street
Columbus, OH 43214
USA
614.447.0906
www.elementville.com
73, 188

ELEPHANT IN THE ROOM
420 N. Liberty Street, Suite 220
Winston-Salem, NC 27101
USA
336.287.3607
www.elephantintheroom.com
48, 100

EMMI
3rd Floor, Unit 17
310 Kingsland Road
London E8 4DB
UK
+44 0 77.5200.1311
www.emmi.co.uk
31

ENTERMOTION DESIGN STUDIO
105 S. Broadway, #800
Wichita, KS 67202
USA
316.264.2277
www.entermotion.com
69, 78, 105

EXHIBIT A: DESIGN GROUP
2-25 E. Sixth Avenue
Vancouver, BC V5T 1J3
Canada
604.873.1583
www.exhibitadesigngroup.com
36, 90

**EXTRACT ASSOCIATED
DESIGNERS**
Driesener Str. 21
Berlin 10439
Germany
+49 30.50.34.11.88
www.extractdesign.com
105

FLAT, INC.
391 Broadway, 3rd Floor
New York, NY 10013
USA
646.613.8833
www.flat.com
160

FOUNDRY CREATIVE, INC.
1425 9th Avenue SE
Calgary, AB T3A4Y7
Canada
403.237.8044
www.foundrycreative.com
27

FRESH DESIGN
20 N. Underhill Station Road
Underhill, VT 05489
USA
802.224.6975
www.freshdesignnow.com
226

FRESH OIL
251 Cottage Street
Pawtucket, RI 02860
USA
401.709.4656
www.freshoil.com
33, 132

FUNNEL: ERIC KASS
1969 Spruce Drive
Carmel, IN 46033
USA
317.590.5355
www.funnel.tv
32, 68, 77

THE GENERAL DESIGN COMPANY
1624 Q Street NW
Washington, DC 20009
USA
202.640.1842
www.generaldesignco.com
112, 127

GEE + CHUNG DESIGN
38 Bryant Street, Suite 100
San Francisco, CA 94105
USA
415.543.1192
www.geechungdesign.com
185, 220

GO WELSH
3055B Yellow Goose Road
Lancaster, PA 17601
USA
717.898.9000
www.gowelsh.com
127, 141, 212

GRAMBLIN DESIGN
1029 E. 41st Street, Suite 23
Tulsa, OK 74105
USA
918.261.2042
176

**GRAPHIC DESIGN STUDIO
BY YURKO GUTSULYAK**
Kharkivske Shose Str. 56
Flat 430
Kyiv 02091
Ukraine
+38 067.446.55.60
www.gstudio.com.ua
185, 189

GRAPHIC MOXIE
2030 Eastwood Road, Suite 1
Wilmington, NC 28403
USA
910.256.8990
www.graphicmoxie.com
225

GRETEMAN GROUP
1425 E. Douglas, Floor 2
Wichita, KS 67211
USA
316.263.1004
www.gretemangroup.com
104, 214, 227

THE HEADS OF STATE
746 South 18th Street
Philadelphia, PA 19146
USA
www.theheadsofstate.com
130

HOET & HOET
Chaussée de Lasne, 42
Rixensart 1330
Belgium
+32 2.646.40.06
www.hoet-hoet.eu
166

¡HOLA CHORIZO!
3149 Blake Street #106
Denver, CO 80205
USA
303.217.3976
www.holachorizo.com
93

HOOK
409 King Street
Charleston, SC 29403
USA
843.853.5532
www.hookusa.com
75, 89, 94, 130

HOTIRON CREATIVE, LLC
5444 E. Galbraith Road
Cincinnati, OH 45236
USA
513.245.8547
www.mwarner.com
104

HYBRID DESIGN
540 Delancey Street, Suite 303
San Francisco, CA 94107
USA
415.227.4700
www.hybrid-design.com
85

ID29
425 River Street
Troy, NY 12180
USA
518.687.0268
www.id29.com
176

ID BRANDING
520 SW Yamhill Street #800
Portland, OR 97204
USA
503.548.6334
www.idbranding.com
84, 95

IMAGEHAUS
12 S. 6th Street, #614
Minneapolis, MN 55402
USA
612.377.8700
www.imagehaus.net
228

ISAAC ARTHUR
3101 Clover Drive
Plainfield, IN 46168
USA
317.403.3173
www.ica-design.net
119

ISOTOPE 221
232 Washington Avenue
4th Floor
Brooklyn, NY 11205
USA
718.783.3092
www.isotope221.com
51

JEFF FISHER LOGOMOTIVES
PO Box 17155
Portland, OR 97217
USA
503.283.8673
www.jfisherlogomotives.com
226

JJ NELSON DESIGNS
953 15th Street, SE
Washington, DC 20003
USA
202.251.1551
174

THE JONES GROUP
342 Marietta Street, Suite 3
Atlanta, GA 30313
USA
404.523.2606
www.thejonesgroup.com
78, 132

KBDA
2452 Wilshire Boulevard, Suite 1
Santa Monica, CA 90403
USA
310.255.0902
www.kbda.com
127

KEVIN AKERS DESIGN +IMAGERY
4095 Lilac Ridge Road
San Ramon, CA 94582
USA
925.735.1015
www.kevinakers.com
109, 112, 126

KONNECT DESIGN
710 Wilshire Boulevard, Suite 404
Santa Monica, CA 90401
USA
310.394.1247
www.konnectdesign.com
39

KORN DESIGN
116 Saint Botolph Street
Boston, MA 02115
USA
617.266.8112
www.korndesign.com
55, 59, 148

KUHLMANN LEAVITT, INC.
7810 Forsyth Boulevard, 2 West
St. Louis, MO 63105
USA
314.725.6616
www.kuhlmannleavitt.com
88

LAM DESIGN GROUP
4812 So. 30th Street, B2
Arlington, VA 22206
USA
703.625.7319
107, 124

LANGTON CHERUBINO GROUP
119 W. 23rd Street, Suite 700
New York, NY 10011
USA
212.533.2585
www.langtoncherubino.com
174

LEWIS COMMUNICATIONS
30 Burton Hills Boulevard
Suite 207
Nashville, TN 37215
USA
615.661.4995
www.lewiscommunications.com
105, 170

LG2BOUTIQUE
3575 Boul. St Laurent
Suite 900
Montréal, QC H2X 2T7
Canada
514.281.8901
www.lg2boutique.com
41, 49, 60, 102–103, 127, 131, 175, 198

LISKA + ASSOCIATES
515 North State Street
23rd Floor
Chicago, IL 60654
USA
312.644.4400
www.liska.com
53, 227

LIZETTE GECEL
4706 Augusta Avenue
Richmond, VA 23230
USA
804.359.1711
156

LLOYDS GRAPHIC DESIGN LTD.
17 Westhaven Place
Blenheim
New Zealand
+64 3.578.6955
167, 208

LOLIGHT DESIGN
2107 Malvern Hill Drive
Austin, TX 78745
USA
512.587.7590
www.lolight.com
76

LOWERCASE, INC.
213 W. Institute Place, Suite 311
Chicago, IL 60610
USA
312.274.0652
www.lowercaseinc.com
31, 50

LUKE DESPATIE
& THE DESIGN FIRM
292 Ridout Street
Port Hope, ON L1A1P7
Canada
416.995.0243
www.thedesignfirm.ca
31, 100, 231

M-ART
7902 Flower Avenue
Takoma Park, MD 20912
USA
301.588.8591
www.m-art.org
130

MARKATOS\MOORE
855 Sansome #101
San Francisco, CA 94111
USA
415.956.9477
www.mm-sf.com
101

MDG
13 Water Street
Holliston, MA 01746
USA
508.429.0755
www.m-d-g.com
224

MINE
190 Putnam Street
San Francisco, CA 94110
USA
415.647.6463
www.minesf.com
24, 165, 218

MIRIELLO GRAFICO
1660 Logan Avenue
San Diego, CA 92113
USA
619.234.1124
www.miriellografico.com
110

MIRKO ILIC CORP.
207 E. 32nd Street
New York, NY 10016
USA
212.481.9737
www.mirkoilic.com
110, 164, 179, 198

MSDS
611 Broadway, Suite 430
New York, NY 10012
USA
212.925.6460
www.ms-ds.com
171, 198, 218

MURILLO DESIGN, INC.
816 Camaron, Studio 216
San Antonio, TX 28212
USA
210.248.9412
www.murillodesign.com
100, 101, 104, 115, 176

**NEOGINE
COMMUNICATION DESIGN**
Level 2, 44 Victoria Street
PO Box 9823
Wellington 6011
New Zealand
+64 4.473.0816
www.neogine.com
155

NIEDERMEIER DESIGN
5943 44th Avenue SW
Seattle, WA 98136
USA
206.351.3927
www.kngraphicdesign.com
47, 78

**NOCTURNAL
GRAPHIC DESIGN STUDIO**
5455 East Ron Rico Road
Cave Creek, AZ 85331
USA
480.688.4207
www.nocturnaldesign.com
153, 229

NOPE ADVERTISING & DESIGN
1582 Portsmouth Place
Mississauga, ON L5M 7W1
Canada
416.904.8523
www.nope.ca
43

OGILVY & MATHER
115 North Duke Street
Durham, NC 27701
USA
919.281.0649
www.ogilvy.com
125

OKAN USTA
47 Belair Road
Staten Island, NY 10305
USA
917.599.6513
www.okanusta.net
114

ONE ZERO CHARLIE
5112 Greenwood Road
Greenwood, IL 60097
USA
815.648.4591
www.onezerocharlie.com
105

OXIDE DESIGN CO.
3916 Farnam Street
Omaha, NE 68131
USA
402.344.0168
www.oxidedesign.com
20, 110, 208

**PARAGON MARKETING
COMMUNICATIONS**
PO Box 6097
Salmiya 22071
Kuwait
+965 5716063
www.paragonmc.com
195

PASSING NOTES
200 2nd Street, No. 201
Oakland CA, 94607
USA
510.835.8035
www.passing-notes.com
87, 142, 144

PAT TAYLOR GRAPHIC DESIGN
3540 S Street NW
Washington, DC 20007
USA
202.338.0962
139, 187, 196

PAVONE, INC.
1006 Market Street
Harrisburg, PA 17101
USA
717.234.8886
www.pavone.net
72

PENCIL
Unit 10, Foxcote Avenue
Bath Business Park
Bath BA2 8SF
UK
+ 44 0 845.290.3930
www.penciluk.co.uk
162

PENGUINCUBE
PO Box 113-6117
Hamra 1103 2100
Beruit
Lebanon
+961 1.740088
www.penguincube.com
173

PENTAGRAM DESIGN
1508 West Fifth Street
Austin, TX 78703
USA
512.476.3076
www.pentagram.com
120, 132, 169

PEOPLE DESIGN INC.
648 Monroe NW, Suite 212
Grand Rapids, MI 49503
USA
616.459.4444
www.peopledesign.com
161

**PINK BLUE BLACK
& ORANGE CO., LTD.**
428 Rama 9 Road, Guanluang
Bangkok 10250
Thailand
+ 66 2.300.5124
www.colorparty.com
20, 115, 147, 154, 163

PITCH CREATIVE
135 Wickham Avenue
Sutton, Surrey SM3 8EB
UK
+44 0 7958.791189
www.pitchcreative.co.uk
28

POULIN + MORRIS, INC.
286 Spring Street, Sixth Floor
New York, NY 10013
USA
212.675.1332
www.poulinmorris.com
35, 164

PRINCIPLE
2412 Bartlett Street, No. 5
Houston, TX 77098
USA
713.521.1625
www.designbyprinciple.com
180

PUBLIC, INC.
10 Arkansas, Suite L
San Francisco, CA 94107
USA
415.863.2541
www.publicdesign.com
38, 172, 177, 194

PUMPKINFISH
3020 NE 32nd Avenue
Suite 303
Ft. Lauderdale, FL 33308
USA
954.563.5690
www.pumpkinfish.com
119

QUALIA
PO Box 5467
Herzliya 46153
Israel
+ 972 0 54.6576572
www.qualiadesign.com
208

RANGE
2257 Vantage Street
Dallas, TX 75207
USA
214.744.0555
www.rangeus.com
115, 170, 218

REACTOR
3111 Wyandotte, Suite 203
Kansas City, MO 64111
USA
816.841.3682
www.yourreactor.com
124, 166

RED DESIGN CONSULTANTS
5 Syngrou Street
Athens 14562
Greece
+30 210.801.0003
www.reddesignconsultants.com
15

RE-GENERATE DESIGN
577 Queen Street W
Toronto, ON M5V2B6
Canada
416.735.5509
www.re-generate.ca
195

RETHINK
700-470 Granville Street
Vancouver, BC V6C 1V5
Canada
604.685.8911
www.rethinkcommunications.com
22, 92, 113, 193

RICKABAUGH GRAPHICS
384 W. Johnstown Road
Gahanna, OH 43230
USA
614.337.2229
www.rickabaughgraphics.com
108, 223

RODRIGO MÁRQUEZ
Teticpac #43 Col. Magdalena
Petlacalco
Mexico City D.F.
Mexico
+52 55.1315.88.41
www.rodrigomarquez.com
209

ROME & GOLD CREATIVE
1305 Tijeras Avenue NW
Albuquerque, NM 87102
USA
505.897.0870
www.rgcreative.com
130, 166, 167

ROYCROFT DESIGN
7 Faneuil Hall Marketplace
4th Floor
Boston, MA 02109
USA
617.720.4506
www.roycroftdesign.com
201

RUBBER DESIGN
375 Alabama Street, Suite 228
San Francisco, CA 94110
USA
415.626.2990
www.rubberdesign.com
210, 221

RUBIN CORDARO DESIGN
115 N. 1st Street
Minneapolis, MN 55401
USA
612.343.0011
www.rubincordaro.com
131

RYAN SMOKER DESIGN
116 E. James Street
Lancaster, PA 17602
USA
717.394.6932
www.ryansmoker.com
124

RYAN RUSSELL DESIGN
2515 Shawn Circle
State College, PA 16801
USA
814.880.6377
136

S DESIGN, INC.
3120 W. Britton Road, Suite S
Oklahoma City, OK 73120
USA
405.608.0556
www.sdesign.com
88

SAGMEISTER, INC.
222 W. 14th Street, 15A
New York, NY 10011
USA
212.647.1789
www.sagmeister.com
205

SCIENTIFIC ARTS
18 Tanard Drive
Braeside Victoria 3195
Australia
+61 422 674 238
www.scientificarts.com.au
131, 176

SK DESIGNWORKS
1831 Chestnut Street, 4 Rear
Philadelphia, PA 19103
USA
215.568.4432
www.skdesignworks.com
113

SKÁKALA
Vlárská 12
Brno 627 00
Czech Republic
+420 602.573.103
www.skakala.cz
33

SLANT INC.
4310 Westside, Suite F
Dallas, TX 75209
USA
214.528.3322
www.slantdesign.com
161, 174

SMOG DESIGN, INC.
1725 Silver Lake Boulevard
Los Angeles, CA 90026
USA
323.668.9073
www.smogdesign.com
150, 208

SOMMESE DESIGN
100 Rose Drive
Port Matilda, PA 16870
USA
814.353.1951
105, 208

SPARK STUDIO
19 Chessell Street
Southbank, Victoria 3006
Australia
+61 3.9686.4703
www.sparkstudio.com.au
178

STEREOTYPE DESIGN
39 Jane Street, 4A
New York, NY 10014
USA
212.414.2744
www.sterotype-design.com
179

STEVEN DREYER DESIGN
3414 Chalmers Drive
Wilmington, NC 28409
USA
910.632.5845
www.stevendreyerdesign.com
108, 173

STEVE'S PORTFOLIO
7829 Devon Street
Philadelphia, PA 19118
USA
215.840.0880
www.stevesportfolio.net
115, 131, 198

STRUCK
159 W. Broadway, Suite 200
Salt Lake City, UT 84101
USA
801.531.0122
www.struckcreative.com
137

STUDIO CREAM DESIGN
141 St. Johns Road
Glebe, NSW 2037
Australia
+61 2.9571.7747
www.studiocreamdesign.com.au
28

STUDIO OUTPUT
2 Broadway, Lace Market
Nottingham NG1 1PS
UK
+44 0 115.9507116
www.studio-output.com
20, 78, 141

SUSSNER DESIGN COMPANY
212 3rd Avenue N., Suite 505
Minneapolis, MN 55401
USA
612.339.2886
www.sussner.com
47, 74, 94, 207, 222

SYNERGY GRAPHIX
210 E. 49th Street
New York, NY 10017
USA
646.442.1002
www.synergygraphix.com
145, 215

TILKA DESIGN
921 Marquette Avenue
Suite 200
Minneapolis, MN 55402
USA
612.664.8994
www.tilka.com
143, 154

TIMBER DESIGN CO.
4402 N. College Avenue
Indianapolis, IN 46205
USA
317.213.8509
www.timberdesignco.com
31, 71

TIM FRAME DESIGN
PO Box 3
Cedarville, OH 45314
USA
614.598.0113
www.timframe.com
66—67, 78, 81, 88, 108, 223

TOKY BRANDING + DESIGN
3001 Locust Street
St. Louis, MO 63103
USA
314.534.2000
www.toky.com
71, 82, 145, 146

TOMKO DESIGN
6868 N. 7th Avenue, Suite 210
Phoenix, AZ 85013
USA
602.412.4002
www.tomkodesign.com
33, 47, 132

DIE TRANSFORMER
Immermannstraße 39
Dortmund NRW 44147
Germany
+49 231.9598.495
www.die-transformer.de
23, 79, 99, 161

TRANSISTOR DESIGN
1183 Rue Saint-Vallier Est
Québec, QC G1K 3R
Canada
418.694.2050
www.transistordesign.com
88

TRUE STORY.
1801 W. Larchmont, Unit 201
Chicago, IL 60613
USA
773.636.8888
www.truestoryinc.com
19

TURNER DUCKWORTH
Voysey House,
Barley Mow Passage
London
UK
+44 0 208.994.7190
www.turnerduckworth.co.uk
33, 181, 218, 226

TURNSTYLE
219 NW Market Street
Seattle, WA 9107
USA
206.297.7350
www.turnstylestudio.com
26

UMS DESIGN STUDIO
3/94 Rajnigandha, D N Nagar
Andheri (West)
Mumbai, Maharashtra 400 053
India
www.umsdesign.com
218

UNCONSTRUCT
133 Florida Avenue
Washington, DC 20001
USA
240.461.8861
www.unconstruct.com
153

UNIT-Y
655 W. Irving Park Road
Suite 2817
Chicago, IL 60613
USA
312.388.8864
www.unit-y.com
105

VALENTINE GROUP NEW YORK
555 W. 25th Street, Floor 3
New York, NY 10001
USA
212.989.8188
www.valentinegroup.com
197

VAUGHN WEDEEN CREATIVE
116 Central SW
Albuquerque, NM 87102
USA
505.243.4000
www.vwc.com
227

WALSH ASSOCIATES
200 E. Broadway, Suite 100
Tulsa, OK 74105
USA
918.743.9600
www.walshbranding.com
230

WEBER SHANDWICK
VISUAL COMMUNICATIONS
1717 Main Street
Suite 1600
Dallas, TX 75201
USA
469.375.0223
www.webershandwick.com
208

WHITE_SPACE
6677 Delmar Boulevard #250
St. Louis, MO 63130
USA
314.880.3800
www.findthewhitespace.com
40

WILLIAM HOMAN DESIGN
111 Marquette Avenue
Suite 1411
Minneapolis, MN 55401
USA
612.869.9105
www.williamhomandesign.com
71, 215

WILLOUGHBY DESIGN GROUP
602 Westport Road
Kansas City, MO 64111
USA
816.561.4189
www.willoughbydesign.com
133

WINK
126 N. 3rd Street, No. 100
Minneapolis, MN 55401
USA
612.455.2642
www.wink-mpls.com
20, 71, 80, 91, 100, 122, 123, 161, 163,
164, 167, 219

WORK LABS
2019 Monument Ave
Richmond, VA 23220
USA
804.358 9372
www.worklabs.com
70, 86

ZYNC COMMUNICATIONS
282 Richmond Street East
Suite 200
Toronto, ON M5A 1P4
Canada
416.322.2865
www.zync.ca
46, 62, 88